Published by National Lampoon Press

National Lampoon, Inc. • 8228 Sunset Boulevard • Los Angeles • CA 90046 • USA • AMEX:NLN

NATIONAL LAMPOON, NATIONAL LAMPOON PRESS and colophon are trademarks
of National Lampoon

National Lampoon Help: by Scott Rubin
Photos by AP, Dreamstime.com, Photos.com, Adobe Stock Photos

p. cm.

ISBN-10: 0978832329
ISBN-13: 978-0978832322
$14.95 U.S. - $18.50 Canada

Cover by
MoDMaN and Sam McCay

Book Design by
Sam McCay

Production by
JK NAUGHTON

COPYRIGHT © 2007 by NATIONAL LAMPOON

ALL RIGHTS RESERVED

PRINTED IN THE UNITED STATES OF AMERICA

This publication contains some factual material presented in a humorous manner. It is intended for entertainment and not as a source of information or as practical advice. If the reader requires personal advice or assistance, a competent professional should be consulted.

The author and the publisher specifically disclaim any responsibility for any liability, loss, or risk, personal or otherwise, which is incurred as a consequence, directly or indirectly, of the use and application of any of the contents of this book.

1 3 5 7 9 10 8 6 4 2

JUNE 2007

WWW.NATIONALLAMPOON.COM

NATIONAL LAMPOON

HELP!

Scott Rubin

TABLE OF CONTENTS

CHAPTER 1: DO YOU NEED HELP? 1
The Great American Help Quiz

CHAPTER 2: MONEY 15
Achieving Your Financial Freedom

CHAPTER 3: DIETING & NUTRITION 31
You're A Fat Guy, Eat!

CHAPTER 4: HOOKING UP 49
The Art of Club Lying

CHAPTER 5: CREATIVITY 69
Finding the Way to Your Creative Bliss

CHAPTER 6: STRESS MANAGEMENT 89
Choosing a New Life Paradigm

CHAPTER 7: LOVE & RELATIONSHIPS 105
Having it All by Letting Her Think <u>She</u> Has it All

CHAPTER 8: MENTAL HEALTH 123
Conquering Depression

CHAPTER 9: ORGANIZATION 143
Decluttering Your Life

CHAPTER 10: SEX 165
How to Explode on Your Terms

CHAPTER 11: LIVING IN THE NOW 185
Enlightenment Through Affliction

CHAPTER 12: THE SEARCH FOR GOD 199
Finding the Lord Almighty

To my kids.

Please don't ever
show this book
to Social Services.

Chapter 1
Do You Need Help?

The Great American Help Quiz

Help. It's a simple word but yet it is the essence of our existence as a species. No man can make it through this insane journey without some. But just how much help does one need? Is it, "You got a light?" or "Can you please light me on fire." Only through the results of this exam can we begin to understand the depth of Help you may require.

Do not get nervous, there is no time limit or proctor and the results will remain with you alone and the guy peering over your shoulder right now.

Be prepared, the truth can sting; I never got over learning that my SAT score was actually lower than my IQ. But don't panic, the pages in this book will allow you to make the proper adjustments so that you may have a long and fulfilling life without ever breaking a sweat – now that's Help!

The Quiz

Circle the correct answers. Check your scores and answers at the end of this chapter.

1. The road to success is much easier if I ...
    A. become a better liar than the new suck-up across the hall
    B. limit my outbursts of total rage to at least once a week
    C. have 3 less drinks at next year's Christmas party
    D. volunteer to be the first one to fall backwards during the trust-building workshop – even though half your co-workers won't catch you
    E. tell my boss I have photographs of him banging the receptionist and I'm about to post them on MySpace
    F. live at home and wait for my parents to die

2. When you're on your daily commute in bumper to bumper traffic, do you feel like...
    A. swerving into oncoming traffic
    B. pulling over and crawling in the back seat in the fetal position
    C. loading up the trunk with C4 and committing Jihad
    D. boning the hottie who keeps cutting you off

E. swinging open your front door into the carpool lane and tripping up one of those Priuses that are blazing by you

F. all of the above

3. Stare at the following photo. What do you see?

A. a woman lying on her side naked with a black mole on her butt

B. a great location for a Starbucks

C. an endless front lawn I have to cut

D. the last place I planted my pot

E. the tallest mountain I shall ever traverse

F. the infinite void of nothingness which is my life

4. How often do you go out with women?

A. Never

B. Twice a year and on Lent

- C. Only when I get a lap dance
- D. Does having dinner with my sister count?
- E. Can it be a guy, I'm not gay… but can it be?

5. What's your first thought after encountering a gorgeous woman at a bar?
    - A. I must go home now and masturbate
    - B. I must get her MySpace page and then go home and masturbate
    - C. God, I hope I trimmed my nose hairs.
    - D. Do I put the roofie in her drink now or wait until she goes to the bathroom?
    - E. If only I ordered "6 Second Abs"
    - F. She's looking right at me and doesn't see me. Wow, I'm invisible! It's a superpower. I can go anywhere and beautiful women don't see me. Hmmm, is that a good thing?

6. When you go to the beach, you immediately…
    - A. cover yourself with sand and pretend to be a sand castle and the entire outlying feudal village
    - B. run as fast as you can into the water and hope you're confused with a sea lion
    - C. Tell everyone you have a series of pre-cancerous skin lesions and need to be confined to under the umbrella, fully wrapped in your Scooby Doo beach towel

- D. Stake claim to the abandoned lifeguard station and pray that no one drowns
- E. Lightly jog down the beach with your shirt off risking that your jiggling mass of flesh won't revolt nearly every beachgoer
- F. Lay your massive girth on the shoreline and invite swimmers to search for shells in between your flesh rolls

7. When you've been at work for at least 5 hours, do you feel...?
   - A. a new respect for your high school guidance counselor who recommended that you become a ward of the state
   - B. defecating on your boss' desk
   - C. stabbing your boss with your letter opener
   - D. running down the hallway with an AK-47
   - E. stealing company office supplies, including: the reception area couch, your desk and your boss' company car
   - F. all of the above

8. Stare at the following photo. What do you see?

   A. A desperate cry for attention
   B. Quite possibly the most annoying sounding *a cappella* group in history
   C. The understudies for the Blue Man Group
   D. A police lineup to identify a headless rapist
   E. My friends
   F. The only guaranteed way to protect yourself from Chlamydia

9. Who do you most fear?
   A. Dick Cheney
   B. Ethan from *Lost*
   C. Your waitress after complaining that your soup is cold
   D. The 6'5" guy standing next to you at the urinal
   E. Ben Affleck in any starring role
   F. My credit report

10. What is the name of the nearest mental facility?
    A. The Henry Mayo Mental Health Sanitarium
    B. Pathways
    C. County Psychiatric Asylum
    D. State Mental Hospital
    E. The Neil Stein Halfway House
    F. You actually know the name of this place?

11. When you go to the All-You-Can-Eat Salad Bar/Buffet do you…?
    A. head to your table with a salad that resembles Mt. Rainier
    B. have an assistant manager assigned to watch you
    C. get thrown out for putting your mouth under the soft-serve ice cream spigot
    D. asked to leave for demanding a 5th serving of the Beefy Meatball Stroganoff
    E. find yourself still eating, even though you're in your car on the way home
    F. finally pass out, shattering the glass sneeze guard

12. When you're writing a screenplay at your local coffee house, do you think…
    A. I can win Sundance

B. I can finish this thing, if only that damn cappuccino maker would just stop already!

C. If I could just get Horatio Sanz attached I know I can get out of Act II

D. My God, I'll still be writing this on a raft after the Arctic ice sheets melt

E. Maybe this is more of a television show

F. All of the above

13. If Disney were to turn you into an animated character, what would you be?

   A. A gay flea
   B. An overly-adorable talking band saw
   C. any sea creature with Robin Williams' voice
   D. a gender-ambiguous raccoon
   E. a selfish kangaroo with a magic pouch
   F. a talking pair of Vans that sound a lot like Andy Dick

14. When you take off your dirty clothes, do you…?

   A. try to incorporate them into the room's décor
   B. leave them in a pile for the house rodents to nest in
   C. give them to the homeless guy down the street
   D. return them to Kohl's for a refund and begin the cycle again
   E. I don't take off my dirty clothes, I just spray

myself with Axe body spray

F. I've considered doing laundry but as long as the whites still have to be separated from darks, I can't, in good conscience, participate

Correct answers:
1. F
2. F
3. E
4. C
5. D
6. C
7. A
8. F
9. C
10. D
11. E
12. D
13. E
14. E

How You Scored:

All 14 correct:

You are a fully-realized human being and require no help. Close the book and pass it down to that turkey next to you

9-13 correct:

You're almost capable of coping in this world but are still holding on to certain societal mores that force you to live your life as if it matters. It doesn't. Let it go: It's free and it requires almost no effort.

5-9 correct:

You need help. You're a lost soul in search of a philosophy – here it is: Give up. Building something can take a lifetime but quitting is instantaneous. The world is filled with happy quitters. We're the ones who float on boats all day and marvel at God's creations. Be a quitter.

1-4 correct:

You're pathetic. How you get through a day is beyond my comprehension. Do you really believe in 30 years anybody is going to care how many famous clients you had or how "ripped" your abs were? Of course not. Don't become one of those pitiful souls on their death bed that utters, with their last dying breath, "if only I had done a lot less and ate a lot more." Start now, and enjoy today.

0 correct:

You are so wound up and over-booked, you probably had your assistant take the test for you or text messaged the answers via your new iPhone. Tell your assistant to put the book down and go back to IMing your palates instructor – you're hopeless.

Chapter 2

Money

In This Chapter...

✔ Work: Man's foolish pursuit

✔ Mom and Pop are your personal ATM

✔ To feel rich is to be rich

Achieving Your Financial Freedom

No one wants to work. It's hard. It's meaningless. And it eats up valuable time from watching *Sports Center*. The mind numbing fluorescents, the cubicles, the bipolar bosses. And at the end of the day, how much have you really made? Your bosses make all the money, you don't.

So why bother?

> *"I can't help but to think that if I had pursued all the ideas I had as a young man, I would have died by 21."*
> — *Thomas Edison*

Getting By — Without Working A Day In Your Life

Recently, I went to a financial analyst and he showed me a chart illustrating how much money I'll need to earn over the next thirty years if I planned to send two kids to college, buy a house, and retire comfortably. It was insane.

By 2030, I'll need $2 million for the kids' college fund, $2 million to pay off the mortgage and equity line on a four bedroom tract home, and $5 million to retire. Then he tells me, "That is why we have to start investing now. We need a game plan." A game plan?! I need an *Ocean's 11* bank heist!

It was so profoundly depressing.

At my current salary, I would have to work fourteen hours a day for the next three decades to pay for kids I don't have, for a stucco house I don't want, and for a retirement that seems so far off, that the thought of the earth ending in thirty years in a feverish Al Gore toxic haze seems more real, and frankly, much more desirable.

Why even live?

Chapter 2: Money

Basically, I would work nearly my entire life, so that for my last 10 years I could be somewhat comfortable.

Here's the reality. At age 80 I'm too far gone to be made "comfortable." I'm being "warehoused" in a suicidally-depressing assisted living facility, everything is going to hurt, I can barely move, I can't get an erection – so what's the point *where* I'm comfortably retired? Either way I'm getting raped, beaten, or robbed weekly by some angry Filipino orderly – no matter if it's some pathetic government institution or a "middle class" Sun City retirement home in Henderson, Nevada.

"If I had known how many times I would be married, I would have been much less successful."
— Donald Trump

The truth is, it's too late for our generation. Shit is just too damn expensive!

Between paying back our student loans, algorithmic variable mortgage rate increases, and monthly health insurance premiums greater than Bel-Air Country Club dues – it's utterly and completely pointless to work!

> *"Walk tall and carry a big stick. That's all you need – I swear."*
> — Barry Bonds

Sure, maybe there was a time when the American Dream seemed achievable, but that was 1955. Houses cost 12 grand. Only the rich went to college. And the only tests the doctor ordered were a tongue dispenser down the throat, a quick look in the ears, and two fingers pressed against the nut sack as you coughed.

Everybody was a conformist square and dutifully died at 65 (so as not to be a burden on society) and there was no retirement. Your "diverse financial portfolio" was a passport savings account at your locally-owned bank – that was your game plan for life.

And you got home at 5:30.

> *"Life is a lot harder when you finally get a real job."*
> — George W. Bush

It's a new world, and even if you wanted your share of the American Dream and were committed to that fourteen-hour work day, it's still a very dicey life choice.

Too Many Wonderful Distractions

Who can work today anyway?

The distractions are so enticing that nobody can resist sloughing off. There are over 40,000 Starbucks alone, and lest we forget, 11 million porn sites; 12,000 horrifying Google news alerts that must be clicked on; the Jack-in-the-Box All Day Breakfast Special; playing the Wii at the pimped-out entertainment demo lounge at Best Buy; the new DVD release of *Happy Days*, Seasons 3 & 4; and a panic run to Cold Stone Creamery. It never ends.

So don't work! Don't ever work!

> "In the final analysis, the ones who spent more time on the internet had better knees."
> — Former Surgeon General C. Everett Coop

Your Financial Strategy for Life

Some things in our society are so obvious, and yet nobody gives them any credence. Your best and perhaps only hope is to sponge off your parents. Remember all the times you were scolded for minor offenses?

Well now it's payback time!

Scrounging off your parents

I'm assuming that you're not destitute because you had enough money to buy this book, and you're literate, which means that you probably were raised by at least middle class parents.

One of the few advantages of being alive today is that many of our parents were financially responsible and productive citizens. They had a "game plan," and it worked for them. And now it's going to work for us.

> "It pays to live in someone else's house. I've never worked a day in my life."
> — Kato Kaelin

You can safely scrounge off your parents for a pretty long time nowadays. Nobody is going to say anything if you take from your folks until age 30. And since 40 is the new 30, you can securely ride the parental gravy train well into middle age – without any stigma attached.

The key to taking from your parents is to know from the get-go that this is going to be your financial strategy for *life*.

There can be no guilt!!!

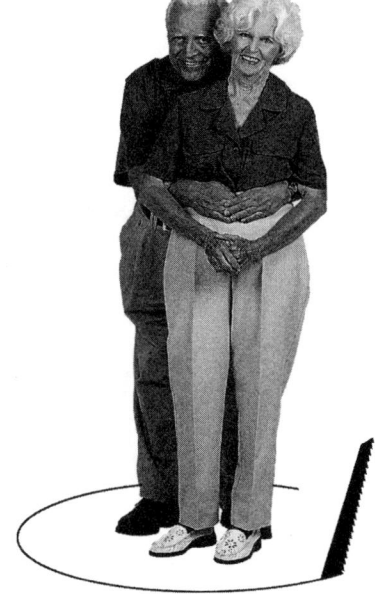

Chapter 2: Money

Look, nobody really wants to take from their parents. They deserve a life. But you didn't ask to be born... they made a choice to bring you into this world. And frankly, isn't it their fault that they raised you to be completely incapable of holding down a job? Aren't they responsible for not teaching you a specific craft or trade (although I'm not sure there's a lot of demand for a blacksmith or cobbler these days)?

Sure, they may have sent you to college, but what is that? How are you supposed to make a living with a major in Third World Cultures and a minor in Bongwater Management?

You can't. You're *fucked!*

Bridging to your inheritance

Okay, so you've been scrounging for years and you're now in your early forties, and yes, you've overheard some relatives muttering at a Bar Mitzvah...

"What a loser."

But really, that's a small price to pay for a twenty year free ride. And who's the loser anyway? Look at these people, they're miserable, working that 14-hour day — while you on the other hand, look great! You've read all the classics, watched all six seasons of *24* on DVD (twice), defeated the two trolls in the lava pit in *Resident Evil 4* and can gleefully rattle off the football and baseball statistics of Bo Jackson.

It's really impressive. You even managed to take a trip around the world with the winnings from your Fantasy Football league.

> *"It's better to not have ever tried at all than to have tried and succeeded"*
> —Kenneth Lay

But now it's getting near the end of your run.

You spotted the *Dr. Spock Baby Book* in the trash one day, hard evidence that your parents are through rationalizing. No more can they say, "Well, if he went to graduate school it would have cost me a fortune!" or "If he had become a doctor, I'd still be paying through the nose!"

As further proof, look at the guest wing off the garage your folks had built for you in sunnier times. In exchange for free rent, you had agreed to maintain it, but two decades of living through your "adolescent phase" have left it in a state of sub-Skid Row disrepair. It's starting to get bad. But there's hope.

Your parents are almost dead.

The average life expectancy for an American male is 75 and for women it's 81. Assuming that your parents had you in their late twenties (the average) that means your father can go at anytime and mother has, at best, only a few years left.

But it gets rosier. Because you've been leeching off them for decades, their accumulated stress level has gone through the roof. By now, Mom and Dad almost certainly suffer from a series of debilitating stress related diseases: Gout, MS, unexplained pain, colitis, and a sundry assortment of just-barely-treatable cancers. Throw in the fact that they haven't had a vacation together since the Carter administration, and your parent's life expectancy is really around 65.

Translation: PAY DAY!

You made it. You get the house, the cars, the bank accounts... all of it. Awright, so you have to split it with your brother, but it's still a pretty good deal. So just take a break from your PSP and pat yourself on the back. You've never worked a day in your life, and now you even have a nest egg to show for it.

Your folks would be proud!

Being Rich

So you've achieved a kind of success – a plateau of sorts – but most people want *more*.

Although a noble pursuit, skating through life without ever filing a tax return is only moderately fulfilling at best. If you're too smitten with the American Dream, if images of fancy cars and a big house with hot-and-cold running prostitutes haunts your every waking moment, then you need a financial strategy

"Success is getting up, looking out, and realizing everything's okay and going back to sleep."
— Punxsutawney Phil

that offers a greater return than you'll ever get selling off your dead parents' Ethan Allen dinette set.

Obviously, work is out of the question, so unless you win the Tri-State Lottery or hook up with Ivanka Trump, you can forget about having anything close to a seven-figure bank account. But don't let that stop you! Get *creative!*

Imagine you're a rich person ten years ago

It's not that long ago.

"I run from success."
— *Barry Sanders or Tiki Barber*

The Simpsons and South Park were on the air, the Yankees had a good team and the Palestinians were fighting the Israelis. You see, it's exactly the same as today, but just a little different. You can use this to your advantage.

Let's say that you desire a rich man's car, perhaps a Jaguar XJ-S. Brand new, it would set you back about 90 grand. However, the same model, just ten years old, now costs about $4000 – and to the untrained eye they look pretty damn close. Okay, so the car doesn't have state-of-the-art navigation or side curtain airbags, but hey, it's a fucking Jag and it's got all that burled walnut and that leaping jaguar chrome hood ornament.

"A person's success is solely dependent on their ability to spell the word success."
— *Daniel Webster*

Chapter 2: Money

Almost nobody can tell the difference, especially people stupid enough to be impressed by these things.

And keep in mind that rich people just ten years ago were in awe of the gadgets and accessories on their glistening new Jag. They bragged about the ABS brakes. They marveled at the single CD/Cassette player. As I recall, even James Bond drove a Jag around this time, so if it was *ever* good enough for 007, it's *still* good enough for a dumpy guy living at home at 35.

Now spread that four grand purchase price over 72 months, and you are one pimpin' rich dude for a mere fifty bucks a month. However, there is one catch:

DO NOT DRIVE THIS CAR! THIS CAR WILL BREAK BEYOND YOUR WILDEST IMAGINATION. THE ENGINE WILL EXPLODE, THE TRANSMISSION WILL CRUMBLE, AND THE ELECTRICAL SHORTS IN THE BLINKERS WILL IGNITE A SERIES OF RECORD BRUSH FIRES THAT WILL BE TELEVISED LIVE FROM THE CHANNEL 7 EYEWITNESS NEWS COPTER AND FOR WHICH YOU WILL ULTIMATELY BE FOUND RESPONSIBLE AND PUBLICLY VILIFIED.

Remember, safety first. Your decade-old Jag is to be used *only* for dates and picking up old friends and relatives from the airport. That's it, nothing more. The rest of the time it should be strategically parked in the driveway just in front of the garage (your house) with a "For Sale" sign on the windshield that clearly states a $62,000 asking price. Your name should be clearly legible on the sign, so that there will be no doubt about who's bringing home the bacon in *this* household.

For *actual* transportation, pick up one of those electric Razor scooters at Toys 'R Us for a hundred bucks and never be seen on it without a full face crash helmet with a blackened visor. And *always* remember to park it behind the garage.

To feel rich is to be rich

The best part of being wealthy is the ability to buy endless amounts of crap whenever you want. Everybody loves to shop, but when you're poor it's really painful to walk around the Bloomingdale men's department.
But shopping is great! And everybody should participate. So put yourself in a position that you are rich.

Make frequent visits to your local 99-Cents store.

You can be the shit, walking around with $10. Buy everything. Walk around the store with the attitutude of a rich person – you're P. Diddy on a bling roll. Tell yourself, "I can buy anything in this store if I want to." Look down at the other customers, the illegal immigrants shopping for foodstuffs and the homeless couple counting their change at the checkout stand. They're "little people" compared to you!

And remember, it's the 99-Cents store, so don't forget to splurge. Show the other customers that you're not here for staples like canned shoulder pork and a case of Shasta strawberry soda... you've got *disposable income* that you're going to spend on tchotchkes and other crap you'll never use or consume! Don't hesitate for a moment to buy those pimento stuffed Bulgarian Olives. Pick up the peculiar half walrus, half-dolphin candlestick holders. Nab that faux crystal Lucite bowl in DayGlo green. You're rich! Filthy rich! So fill up that shopping cart and go go GO!

> **"Look at me, I own nothing and nobody could be more successful than me."**
> —*Jesus H. Christ*

This is your moment to shine and let the world know that you've *arrived*.

In Conclusion

To be honest, I'm having a little trouble finishing this chapter. I think I've taken my own advice to heart. I've lost all motivation to continue writing. What's the point?

You know, finances are a funny thing. Money and material possessions are great, but at the end of the day it's just way too much effort for the amount of joy they ultimately return.

I'd rather take a nap.

Chapter 3
Diet & Nutrition

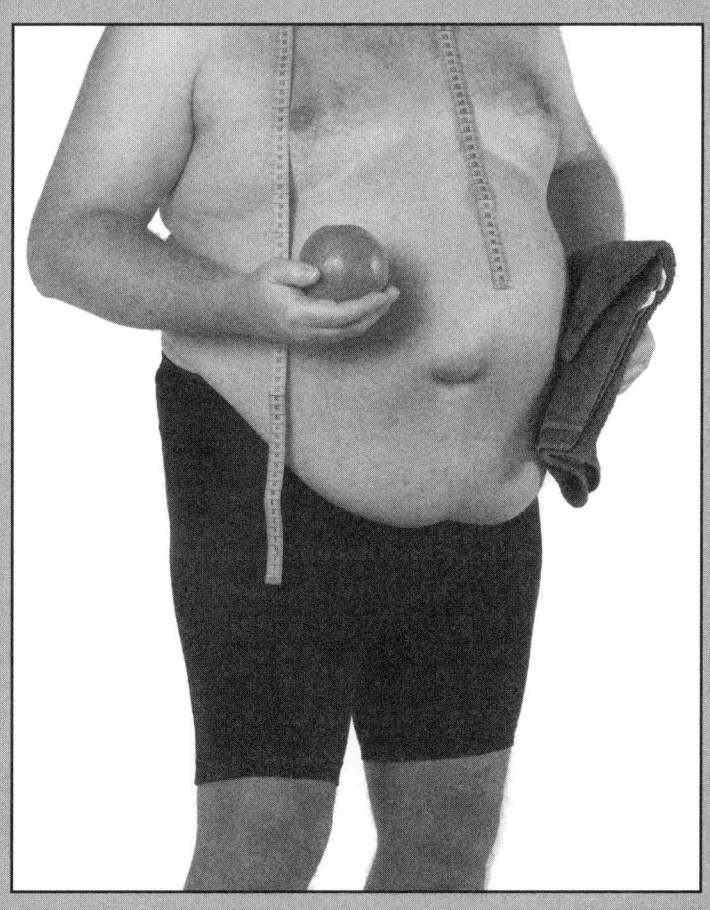

In This Chapter...

✔ It's a Fat Guy Nation

✔ How the stout find women

✔ Dropping 20 by contracting a stomach virus

You're a Fat Guy – Eat!

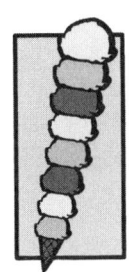

So this is not how you imagined going through life, the same weight as Al Gore, but hell, you're eating Breyer's Cookies 'n Cream right now!

Life is *good*.

You have pizza for breakfast and the Shakey's All-You-Can-Eat Buffet for lunch. You're much warmer than most people. You're cute. You're lovable. You're bouncy. Enjoy it!

Embracing The Starving Inner Child

Don't let the Stick People scare you – they're always trying to convince you that you suffer from low self-esteem and need to drop 80 pounds. I don't see drive-thru salad places. During the Super Bowl, when the entire world is watching, are they advertising celery stalks? Of course not — it's burgers, fries, chips, beer, candy and soda. On your birthday, do they come out with a giant salad with burning carrot sticks? No! It's Double Chocolate Fudge Dream Cake.

"God must be fat because he created us in his own image."
— *Jerry Falwell*

Fat or thin. Society overwhelms us with mixed signals about what to eat, but this much is clear...

This is your world.
It's made for you. You belong!

You just need to accept it. Don't fight it anymore, relish in it.

Drive down any boulevard in your town and there it is: KFC right across the street from Wendy's, which is right across the street from Jack-in-the-Box, which is right next door to Pizza Hut. I mean c'mon, every one of us lives in a fuckin' food court! Can it get any better! The world is designed for fat people and all we do is fight it, rack ourselves with guilt. You must stop right now!

This is the greatest time in the history of man to gorge ourselves. We don't even have to get out of the *car*.

FAT FACTS:

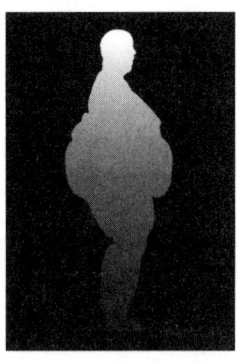

> Roger Ebert outlived Siskel despite being 100 pounds heavier than him.

> Biggie Smalls did not die of an obesity-related illness

> Jackie Gleason lived to the ripe old age of 70 and chain smoked.

> Dom Deluise is still alive... I think.

Chapter 3: Diet & Nutrition 35

In what other moment in time could you get your paws on a McNugget? Even just seventy years ago it wasn't possible. You would have to raise a chicken, debeak it, put it in a cage and fill it with hormones. But you would never find the hormones because pharmaceutical companies hadn't isolated them yet. You would then have to build some sort of factory where they somehow would reconstitute the chicken. But no one in the 1930's would even know what the word "reconstitute" meant. Yet now we have reconstituted chicken! And then there's the deep frying, the breading, the chemicals that go into the Honey Mustard Sauce! It never ends, and that's just the McNugget!

> "Americans are getting too heavy. I can imagine a point when the Earth can't take all the extra weight and falls off its axis and goes spiraling through our solar system, eventually entering Jupiter's gravitational field and becoming its next moon. But even with that dire scenario, I still can't resist the new McDonalds Third Pounder with Cheese."
> — Al Gore

Run outside right now and scream to your God, "Thank you for letting me be born in America in the latter half of the 20th Century! And thank you for those electric sit-down shopping carts at Walmart!" This is our world. It's made for us, not them.

You want self esteem. Hundreds of companies construct buildings for us with large colorful signs, and large seats and backlit fast food menus... They care about us. They are our grandmother preparing a big family feast times 1000. Many of them sit around each day, spending billions on how to satisfy us... and they do: Jack-in-the-Box Curly Fries, Wendy's Chili, the Shamrock Shake, Cinnabon, the Buffalo Chicken Wing Pizza! Let it in.

This is a fat guy's world! EAT!!!!

Exercise program

Forget it! You are in the best shape of your life!

I am tired of the angry Stick People people telling us fat folk that we need to work out and get in shape.

Why... so I can become one of them? A starving, cranky, little thin person, who does nothing but work out, talk about not eating, and work out some more – that's a life?!

And they're wrong, very wrong!

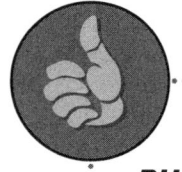

RULE OF THUMB:

› Wherever you see a fat guy, there is a completely buffed thin guy just underneath.

On the average, fat people burn more calories than thin people and they're much stronger. Try carrying the equivalent of a baby grand piano on your back 24 hours a day. There are also tremendous strength training benefits to this kind of severe resistance exercise. Did you ever see the calves on a fat guy? They're huge! Thin people must constantly lift weights to build this kind of body strength, whereas fat guys just have to walk up a single flight of stairs to maintain their awesome power.

The reality is, that if you're pushing 250, you're working out 24 hours a day. So it maddens me when the Stick People will say "Go to the gym... You should get in shape." Shape?! Are you kidding me, I'm doing leg presses right now, pal! And you're just standing there mouthing off.

Shut up and eat something!

Chapter 3: Diet & Nutrition

37

Workout tips for the fat guy

Sure we can do more, no one wants to get into the 400's and beyond and have to be cut out of his apartment with a chainsaw. But you must be careful your body is already stressed by your natural workout.

"Not eating... is not an option"
— *Orson Welles*

Look, you're gonna gain, you just want to keep it at a *moderate* level.

Here are some stay-active suggestions that won't in any way impede on your Fat Guy lifestyle. Follow them and any future weight gain will be slow and relatively steady:

✔ Don't use the drive-thru. Get out of the car and walk inside the McDonalds

✔ Chew more. A couple of extra bites can give you a good burn

✔ Your daily walk: keep the couch as far away from the cupboards, fridge, or bathroom.

✔ Take a survey lap around the food court before choosing your spot – an excellent cardio workout before your afternoon gorge

✔ Wash the hard-to-reach places on your body. This will give you a wonderful stretch that will burn those extra calories

✔ Fidget

Coping Methods in a World Obsessed with Six-Pack Abs

Although this might be our world, there are still disadvantages to being a Fat Guy in our society. The images of glistening, buffed men, with ripped abs wearing only thongs has come to dominate our culture. Hollywood movies glorify this new American Ideal with the same fervor as Hitler promoting his chiseled Aryan man.

We don't even have funny fat guys in our movies anymore. It's as if they killed them all off! Where are the Gleasons, Farleys, Belushis? Are we willing to sacrifice even comedy for this new homoerotic, image of the American male!

"I would walk a mile for a pizza but not for my health."
— Dr. Phil

Ideally, Fat Guys should let it all hang out, but our society, unfortunately, won't let us. We're made to feel as if we should never take our shirt off at the beach or on a hot summer day at the park. Somehow the only place where it is appropriate while standing in the bleachers, in the dead of winter, wildly screaming with a giant "We're No. #1" painted on our chest. But don't despair, this is only a temporary problem. Eventually all Americans will be fat and there will be no one left to give us those derisive stares.

"Now that I think about it, I'd rather be fat than gaunt."
— Al Roker

But in the meantime, you must attempt to look as thin as possible.

Chapter 3: Diet & Nutrition   39

Problem: "Thin is In"

Best hope for a Fat Guy is to look ambiguous. This can easily be accomplished by wearing extremely baggy clothes – no one will really be able to tell. "Is he fat? or "Is he thin?" The guarded secret of your massive girth remains with you.

> *"At one point I was pushing 300 and no one could tell."*
> — Mahatma Gandhi

However, people are becoming hip to the tent look. It's very much like wearing a baseball cap: everyone knows you're bald under there.

Don't despair, it's still an effective strategy — it just needs a better underlying concept to keep them guessing.

Remember, this is magic. The more committed you are to performing the illusion, the more believable it becomes. Go get 'em, Copperfield.

Solution: A "fat friendly" lifestyle!

Other than walking around with a Guinness-league morbidly-obese fat friend who is *so* fat he makes you look like Lance Armstrong, there's no better way to fool the public than by working in a field that requires wearing a very large, baggy uniform. No one will ever suspect that you're hiding your tonnage because your career demands that you cover yourself in a *sheet*.

Career Choices for the Self-Conscious Fat Guy

— Guaranteed to Conceal!

Become an Esteemed College Professor

You must conduct all your lectures in a large, black doctoral gown. These garments are so baggy, that even if you get out of breath while wheeling in a slide projector, your students will more than likely write it off to a bout of emphysema than to the massive poundage neatly concealed under the black body curtain.

Join the Choir at your Local Church

Make sure it's a choir that sings in those enormous, blinged-out choir robes. You can be 600 pounds under there and not a single parishioner will ever suspect you broke the Second Deadly Sin of Gluttony.

Chapter 3: Diet & Nutrition

Become a Supreme Court Justice

Does anybody really know how enormous any of our Supreme Court Justices are? Who knows how fat Judge Scalia is underneath that endless yarn – he could be pushing 400.

Join Your Local KKK Chapter

This is an excellent choice, especially if you live in some sections of Arkansas and Oklahoma where you'll be able to wear the large white cape 24/7. The hood adds additional cloaking for any Fat Guy that needs to conceal 3 chins or more.

Become the Pope

It's not an easy job to land, but if you can pull it off, it is quite possibly the best career choice for a Fat Guy. They never, ever take that robe off. Never. Pope John Paul II went mountain climbing in it – it's true, look it up.

National Lampoon *HELP!*

Holy Shit, I'm 250 Pounds! Where Can I Get Laid?

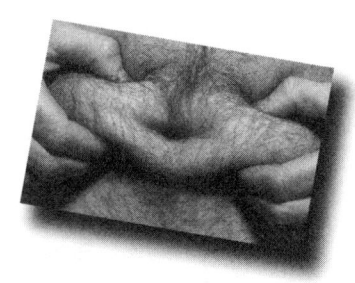

Kmart.

Walk through any Kmart, peer down any aisle and look at the mass of humanity that is actually bigger and more disgusting than you.

You are a greek god at Kmart!

"I haven't chosen food over women. I've chosen men over women."
— Nathan Lane

Sure you have a 44 waist, but at Kmart that's a medium. You're *svelte*. The people that go to Kmart are all the people that couldn't figure out to go to Walmart. They're ugly *and* they're stupid and you, well, you are hopefully just a little chunky around the waist, with adorable love handles.

Making the move

There is no use trying to pick up on the store's patrons – it's a lost cause. You'll be going after the checkout ladies. At least one out of every ten Kmart checkout ladies is a solid "7" and that includes the three old ladies with the purple hair. There's always at least one hottie in the bunch. Now, Kmart's best sees nothing but 1's and 2's all day. Their eyes are conditioned to see only the bottom of the human gene pool. But then you walk up, hopefully a solid 4 or better… bam.

"I'm not fat!"
— *Tyra Banks*

You're *Sanjaya!*

Now pick your cashier strategically. Stand back and search — find the 7.

You found her.

When you approach, you'll see the twinkle in her eyes. This is your moment. The vision of a 4 or 5 (you) will be like looking at a beautiful rainbow. You have never looked so good to a person. She begins to flirt with you. This is a checkout girl's mating call!

Listen to the signals:

HER: *"I hope you found what you were looking for?"*

YOU: *"Yes, I did* (look her in the eye)*... and you?"*

That's it. That's all it takes. Go ahead and slip her your business card.

Here's another scenario:

HER: *"And how was your shopping today at Kmart?"*

YOU: *"It just became* (again, make eye contact) *...much better."*

If you receive either one of these lines, you're in.

The checkout lady at Kmart will never say anything other than "Price check," "Thank you for shopping at Kmart," or "Can you please swipe your card again" – that's it. Any other dialogue means that she wants you and wants you badly.

It takes very little from that point on to pick her up. Really anything will do – they don't have to be the lines above. A simple, "Maybe you can write your name and number down on the back on my receipt and we can go out sometime." Don't say anything more. It's not necessary.

You're *IN*.

Chapter 3: Diet & Nutrition   45

When You Absolutely Need To Drop 20

There is only one time in a man's life that requires actual weight loss: Attending Family Events.
It's just such a hassle. Your dad, your brother, constantly ribbing and mocking you. And there you are, pretending your not interested in seconds and thirds and that you have no room for dessert. Then there's the after-dinner intervention. You'd rather not deal with it. So this is what you do.

Lose weight thru botulism!

There is only one sure way to lose weight when you're a Fat Guy and that's to get sick. You must contract the stomach flu. There is simply no other reliable way to fight the onslaught of the myriad of tasty temptations.

And it's guaranteed to work!

To pick up a virus that will make you violently ill, simply eat a hot dog in front of any home improvement warehouse; preferably the hot dog stands in front of Lowes or Home Depot. Within 24 hours you'll be projectile vomiting. You're guaranteed to go at least three days without eating with an additional three more days to allow for the slow re-introduction of solid foods. By this time, you might have lost twenty pounds in a week. It's great! Next time you're at the family dinner, you'll

"I eat to live and live to eat. So someone please kill me already."
— *Ariel Sharon*

be eating like a normal fat guy again. People will be amazed at your food consumption without being morbidly obese.

More sources of food borne illness

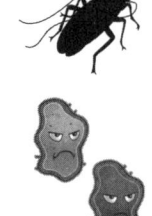

- ✔ Any hamburger place that is combined with a donut shop and is run by a family of angry Asian immigrants

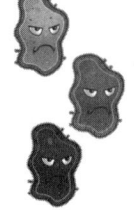

- ✔ Any sushi place that is going out of business

- ✔ Any Indian restaurant that has no customers during the lunch rush

- ✔ Any Jewish deli that serves ham

- ✔ Any restaurant that advertises "World Famous" on their sign

- ✔ Any Burger King that still has its 1980s decor

Years from now, inducing the stomach bug will be part of medical science; much like going to a doctor for botox injections is now. Botox is botulism injected in the face. One day Doctors will prescribe botulism pills so that we won't ever have to patronize these revolting eateries ever again.

"Pouring Carvel soft-serve vanilla onto a steaming hot Cinnabon has to be the greatest tasting experience since Adam bit into the apple."
— *Me (author)*

Dangerous? You bet. But it's gotta be safer than gastric bypass surgery, and it involves no stapling.

In Conclusion

I'm not saying being fat doesn't have its problems. Sure, it's embarrassing to break a chair in half and fall on your ass at your best friend's wedding, but not nearly as embarrassing as catching the Nicole Richie-thin bride hurling up her wedding cake in the back of the banquet hall so her bustier doesn't rip apart during Hava Nagila. Now that's embarrassing. Being fat is our American right as long as you can still have sex and leave your house without the assistance of the Channel 9 news team and a construction crew. You need to revel in it.

Chapter 4

Hooking Up

In This Chapter...

- ✔ Turning bullshit into babes
- ✔ Convert your personal liabilities into perceived assets
- ✔ Have sex like a celebrity

The Art of Club Lying

So now you're in full slack mode, but something seems to be missing. The late night binges at Dunkin' Donuts followed by the usual three rounds at bigroundass.com is starting to wear thin.

And quite frankly, it's becoming embarrassing. The last time you booted up your laptop at Starbucks, a hi-res jpeg of a woman's ravaged ass filled the screen, along with a flashing, Vegas-style pop-up reminder to renew next month's "Adult Friend Finder" subscription. What's more, the accompanying maximum-volume audio of a particularly orgasmic girl-girl muff dive didn't exactly endear you to that cute barrista you were planning to hit on.

Okay, it happens. But now it's time to move on. The need to propagate is more powerful than any digitally induced sexual ecstasy or glazed cruller induced coma. You need to connect with live warm flesh, not 72 dpi pixels.

Don't despair, there is a way, even for a born loser like you, to "hook up". And it's surprisingly easy.

Here's the key:

Lie! Lie! Lie!

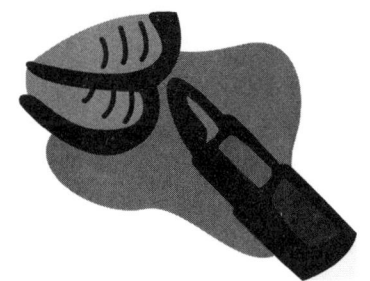

No one is telling the truth, so why should you?

Everybody lies when they go on a weekend sex prowl. Women lie constantly, they just don't think of it as lies. What the hell is make-up? Inflatable push-up bras? That fake tanning spray? Hair extensions? Lip gloss? These are bold face lies. Brunettes are blondes, blondes are brunettes. The drapes never match the carpet.

And guys, what do *we* have? Half of us are still dressed in the grunge era. Unlike women, we've got almost nothing to work with when it comes to

BIG LIE FACTS

› Bill Clinton lied, but now earns up to $650,000 per speech

› George Bush lied about weapons of mass destruction, but was elected for another four years

› Richard Nixon lied, but ended up a respected elder statesman and advisor

› George Washington lied about cutting down a cherry tree, but is now on the dollar bill

seducing the opposite sex. And we have to work *fast* – an hour or two at most before last call. The odds are stacked against us, so how will we ever pass our seed into the 21st Century?

Simple. You lie.

"If not for one good lie and two good drinks, the human race could not repopulate itself."
— Stephen Hawking

Now you say, "What about the ethical questions?" "I don't want to lie. Lying is a sin."

Okay, look, lying is a sin, but you're out there clubbing. This isn't exactly Ten Commandments turf. All biblical rules are disavowed as soon as you walk past the bouncer and flash your fake ID.

And who's speaking the truth in a club anyway? The bullshit is a mile high and twice as deep. In fact, the whole place is built on bullshit. The club's management parks those Ferraris and Porsches out front to make you think you've arrived at an exclusive watering hole for the rich and famous. But c'mon, the Ferrari belongs to the sleazeball club owner and the slick new Porsche belongs to the creepy old guy in the corner – who you pray doesn't come up to you again and recite the Top Ten list from the Urban Dictionary.

Now unless you're a total stud muffin, nothing is going to give you more game than a good old fashioned lie. But dishonesty requires discipline, and a wrong move can quickly turn you from player to played. So listen up and pay attention.

The continuation of our species depends upon it!

The Bullshit Artist

This term has an negative connotation but it really shouldn't. When it comes to hooking up, bullshitting is an actual art form, as much as sculpting, painting, or bonsai gardening.

Like a true artist, the Bullshit Artist possesses the *paint*, the *brush* and the *canvas*. In order to succeed, he must deftly employ all three in perfect harmony.

Here's how:

Case Study: my intern at National Lampoon

OK, here's your chance to witness a true Bullshit Artist at the top of his game.

In reality, my intern, John, is on the lowest rung of the employee food chain at National Lampoon. He looks average, earns zilch, and dresses like a depression-era hobo. He has a National Lampoon business card with his name on it, but no title. That's it. The brutal truth is that without some kind of *Sun-Tzu* battlefield deception, John would never, ever get the opportunity to hide the salami in the Darwinian meat markets of Hollywood, where money and power are king.

> *"Meeting women is easy; waiting for STD results is hard."*
> —Orlando Bloom

But watch how John uses these feeble tools to leverage his options and score...

The Paint: a germ of truth

When John meets and strikes up a conversation with a cute actress/model/whatever at a club, at some point he will remark that he works at National Lampoon. Her eyes will light up, and of course she will ask him, "What do you do there?" and this is where the brush comes in...

The Brush: expanding on the germ

John will say, "I work in motion pictures" (much more impressive sounding than "movies") Now in reality, John's only connection to the National Lampoon movie division is that he occasionally reads scripts for me because I'm too lazy to read them myself. But John has another germ of truth to lay on the table, another brilliant color swatch from his limited palette.

> "Asking a woman out is as simple as ordering food. Just say the dish you want and wait till it comes over."
> — Meatloaf

She'll say, "Wow, what movies have you worked on?"

Okay, now it gets a little tricky, but this is where the master's brush strokes transcend into *art*.

John replies, offhandedly, "Oh, I'm developing new films for Q4."

> *"It's not easy meeting women when you're out of work. You must rely solely on the grace of God and your own fallacious oratory."*
> —Abraham Lincoln

Now did you see that? Word choice is everything. In Hollywood, the term developing is basically just "white noise" – it doesn't mean anything but sounds impressive to doe-eyed neophytes just off the bus from Des Moines. And the use of "Q4" is the fucking clincher. To a novice, any non-accountant who peppers his show biz lingo with references to quarterly business cycles has got to be the real deal, but when you refer to your company's fiscal calendar in hip, abbreviated corporate-speak... man, you're the shit!

One good thing about this approach is that John has not actually lied. So for any of you conflicted Baptists, Orthodox Jews, or former US Presidents planning to follow this example, you're still good. My intern did in fact read a script. National Lampoon does look for scripts (please don't send any) and it could have been for Q4 (fourth quarter) of the year.

> *"I'd rather live in a world with gorgeous dames and no love than a world with love and women that only look like Gertude Stein."*
> —Donald Rumsfeld

No lies, just wonderfully unvarnished bullshit, verbal brushstrokes that help even out the playing field in clubland. Men, this is our lip gloss. It's our hair extensions. It's our push-up bra. Yessir, we're going blonde tonight!

Now, we're *even!*

Chapter 4: Hooking Up   57

 ## The Canvas: a pimped-out vision of you

Now, let's stand back and admire the masterwork that John has created, as seen through the eyes of his tipsy and tragically gullible young victim:

 *"A young guy...borderline cute...making it big in Hollywood movies...he must be some kind of wunderkind...the next Sascha Cohen or maybe one of those new internet comedy geniuses that National Lampoon brought in...he could be rich or on the fast track to something, like, really really awesome."*

(Translation: Fuck me! Fuck me! FUCK ME!)

It's that easy, and no, you don't have to be a National Lampoon quasi-slave to pull this shit off. Any grain of truth can be spun into a glorious George Clooney-like portrait of YOU and projected into the gin-soaked cranium of any young hottie you desire. Or at least the ones who like gin.

So go forth and conquer... you are now a bonafide *Bullshit Artist*.

Bullshit Artist Conversion Table

Use the following table to convert your personal liabilities into perceived assets:

PATHETIC JOB		INTRIGUING CAREER
Jack n' the Box Cook	=	Continental Cuisine Chef
7-11 assistant manager	=	Linguistics Specialist
Dominos Pizza Deliver Guy	=	NASCAR Trainee
Wetzels Pretzels Maker	=	Contortionist
Guy in Rat Suit at Chuck E. Cheese	=	3-D Animation Producer
Living in Your Parents' Basement	=	Financially Independent
Drug Dealer	=	Drug Dealer

OBSESSIVE COMPULSIVE RITUALS		STRIKING INTERESTS
Playing World of Warcraft	=	Expert on Medieval Warfare Methodologies
Sleeping During the Day	=	Out of Body Astral Traveler
Fantasy Football	=	NFL talent scout for new online venture
Writing the same screenplay for 6 years	=	Writer
Masturbating	=	Learning to love myself

Chapter 4: Hooking Up

> *"The only time I ever tell the truth in a bar is when I order a drink."*
> — Bill Clinton

Now if you want to get more adventurous and go after the absolute, most smoking hot young woman in the club, you'll have to ratchet up your game to the next level.

To play among the stars, you must *become* a star...

The Big, Bold Sit-Com Level Lie

You need to pick a whopper that is so over the top that nobody would ever question it. To most people, it would be unimaginable that any human being could possibly lie at such a stratospheric level, and/or stoop to such a subterranean low.

This lie is so big that most women – even the really smart ones who are hip to every known guy trick – cannot assimilate this information as anything but an amazing truth.

So what is this perfectly formed, gargantuan lie?

Pretend you're a big, rich, famous fuck!

I've only done this once but it was completely effective.

Everyone looks *almost* like someone famous. It's true, just think about it. Someone in your life has said to you, "You know, you kinda of remind me of (musician, football player, actor, politician)_____."

Well, now it's your time to cash in on this magnificent genetic coincidence.

For me it was Billy Joel. Years ago, I had an entire club in Miami believing I was him. It was amazing. I signed autographs. I had bottles of Dom Perignon sent to my table. And unimaginable hotties were coming on to me even though just a few weeks earlier, in the same club, I was invisible to them! It was incredible – until it got out of control (the Mafiosa running the club wasn't thrilled by my charade, but more on that later).

You would be amazed at how possible this really is. Follow the guidelines, avoid the pitfalls, and you too can hitch your wagon to a star.

Hey, it worked for me.

Billy Joel
Circa 1980

The Author
Circa 1980

Chapter 4: Hooking Up   61

National Lampoon

Presents

How to Impersonate a Celebrity

...and Score The Hottest Chick in the Club!

A Step-by-Step Guide to a Night of Pure Debauchery
by Scott Rubin

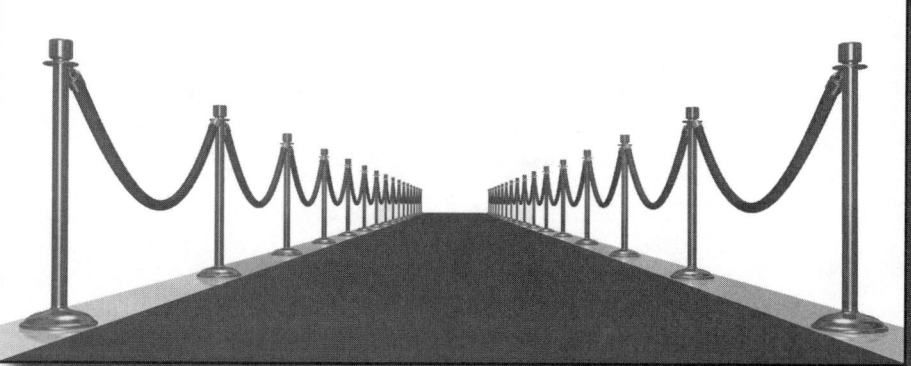

STEP 1: CHOOSE WISELY

Most people look like a few different people. Make sure you pick a celebrity that hasn't been exposed on TV often enough for people to quite make them out. Football players and musicians are perfect.

Football players usually have their helmets on most of the time, so in theory, if you kind of resemble them, you're good. Plus, if you're a fat guy, and you're having trouble coming up with a match, you can easily become an NFL offensive lineman, any NFL offensive lineman. There's not a person on earth that can identify any one of those faces, including their coaches.

Musicians are always good because they aren't on TV enough to be sure exactly what they look like. And when they are being broadcast, they're usually gyrating, jumping around, and making scrunched-up "oogly-oogly" faces at every overwrought guitar riff, so it's kinda hard to make them out.

Remember, clubs are dark, very dark, and of course there's always lotsa drinking going on, so if you only "sorta kinda" look like the famous person whose identity you've hijacked, that should be enough. But you have to be careful in this hi-def age. Don't pick a celebrity with so much public awareness that most people know which nostril, ear, or eyebrow is pierced, which arm has the "Angelina 4-Ever" tattoo laser removal scars, or whose Lakers point guard height conflicts with your five-foot-seven frame.

STEP 2: AN ACTOR PREPARES

Remember, you are now a public figure. People will talk to you as if you are that guy and you must be prepared. When I was Billy Joel, I knew most of his songs, some of his background, and more or less how he dressed. I was comfortable in the role. However, even with some preparation, I still managed to overlook a key Billy Joel characteristic and it nearly cost me my life.

During the evening, when the charade was in full swing, I was approached by the 300 lb. Sicilian club owner, who extended his massive, furry hand and politely (if firmly) asked me if I might play a little something on the club's baby grand piano.

By that time, Don Vito had comped me and my friends (i.e. Billy Joel's entourage) well over $1000 in food and drink. Needless to say, I don't play the piano, so the fear factor was starting to build. Thinking on my feet, I told the owner that I just wanted to relax and enjoy a night on the town with my younger brother, who in reality was my best friend Joel Richman. A shaky excuse, but Sasquatch appeared to buy it at first. However, the ruse collapsed when I absent-mindedly introduced my "younger brother" to him as Joel Joel.

It was a Code Red!

Suddenly an air of suspicion befell the room. Soon faces of adoration quickly turned to scorn and even murderous rage! Needless to say, my "posse" and I vacated the premises posthaste, and to this day there are parts of South Florida that I dare not enter – all because I failed to prepare.

In hindsight, the piano thing would have been an easy fix — a splint on my finger would have done the trick. And the "Joel Joel" fuckup? Two or three less drinks and I shouldn't have mixed in the 'ludes.

STEP 3: EVERY STAR NEEDS AN ENTOURAGE

No celebrity arrives at a club without an entourage.

As you prepare for a night of Studio 54-era debauchery, remember to recruit a couple of friends you can trust as your loyal and submissive posse. To reinforce the illusion, they must agree to take arbitrary and capricious orders from you. As the night wears on, they may find your behavior to be unnecessarily demeaning and degrading, especially when your adopted persona goes so far beyond the act that you actually become the first class celebrity asshole you've chosen to mimic.

"Get me a drink! Hey, get me a drink now!"

"Go ask that girl to come over here, no not that one, the other one, are you an idiot?! Do I have to do everything around here?!"

"Did you hear me? I said bring the car around!"

To avoid a mutiny and possible exposure, and to ensure that you get to enjoy all the "Roman orgy" perks of the celebrity you're impersonating, you must emphasize to your posse beforehand that if everyone plays their part, there will be plenty of leftovers for everybody. That includes sloppy seconds on the half-naked Edie Sedgwicke clone passed out on the men's room toilet.

STEP 4: LET THEM KNOW YOU'RE COMING

Have one of your peeps call ahead to the club's reservations desk and say you'll be arriving, but that it "must be kept secret" and that you'll need a discreet booth in a dark corner "so as not to be recognized." This adds credibility to your visit and will of course guarantee that every nineteen-year-old fuck puppy within a fifty-block radius will know of your presence and form a beeline to your table.

STEP 5: RECRUIT AN INSIDER

It's a long night, and doubters will inevitably emerge, including possibly some friends or relatives of the real celebrity whose public life you've usurped. If you're smart, you will have recruited an insider to stoke the flames, keep an eye out for trouble, and extend the lie until the wee, wee hours. Almost anybody will do. A bus boy, a bartender, a doorman, a cook. This could save your life or at least buy you another hour to close the deal with the hottie in the red dress.

National Lampoon *HELP!*

STEP 6: REMEMBER THE MISSION

Many people will come up to you throughout the evening and ask you to sign autographs, take pictures with them, and dance. The ego rush will be overwhelming. Don't allow your false, inflated sense of self to distract you from your primary objective: to pork the hottest babe of your entire life, if only for a single night and under a criminally false pretense.

STEP 7: THIS PLAYER'S GOTTA RUN

Survey the club for the exit doors. If things go bad, they'll go really bad, really fast. You must have an escape plan, and perhaps a bottle of pepper spray.

As one last precaution, never carry an ID with your actual name, so that if you're killed, the evening newscasts will erroneously report on the death of the real celebrity.

What the hell, you might as well go out with a bang.

Chapter 4: Hooking Up

In Conclusion

Hooking up isn't easy for the "life challenged." It requires bold, out-of-the-box thinking and a dedication to become something you are not. The timid souls among us may be uncomfortable with this approach, but I promise you, after a night with one glistening, tan, blonde named Traci, you'll head back to your job at IHOP with a spring in your step, a new sense of purpose, and a contract out on your life.

Chapter 5

Creativity

In This Chapter...

✔ Devaluing your creative dream

✔ Blending your artistic pursuit with Tostitos

✔ Artistic success through drug abuse

Finding the Way to Your Creative Bliss

"I'm working on a novel, well it's more of a screenplay, actually it's a multimedia live show."

"I'm the best karaoke singer in this town, but American Idol won't come to Saskatchewan."

"You know, it's not quite a live show, some parts are on tape and it has animatronics and stuff."

"By God, I can make it! No one is better with Hand Puppets, no one. It's just really hard to keep them clean."

"I know I could become the world's greatest Bar Mitzvah DJ but where do I get my start? Nebraska has almost no Jews."

"You know, now that I think about it, I think it's more of a novel."

Oh, the endless, nauseating rants of the frustrated creatives.

Okay, we know, you're working on it. Getting the portfolio together, working on a plan, just one more rewrite, one more rehearsal. Awright, Awright, enough already!!!!

"But this is my bliss!"

"This is why I was born, to share my gift to the world!"

"I'm following my dream!"

First of all, stop that bullshit right now! If it was your "bliss," you would be doing it every morning like the way you scroll through your favorite internet-sex-portal-site until you discover yet another sexual fetish that curiously arouses you.

"Art is the only noble quest for man."
—**Mary Kate & Ashley**

"It's my bliss!" — *I laugh at you!*

Get a grip! Do me a favor and look up from your navel gazing for just a minute and acknowledge a few revelations about your...uh...*calling*.

Chapter 5: Creativity **73**

Revelation #1
You Give It Too Much Importance

That's your first mistake: You'll never accomplish your creative dream if you sincerely believe "it's the reason why I was put on this earth."

If you are to succeed, you need to make your great creative pursuit the *least* important part of your dismal life.

Okay, the truth!

Masturbation gives me plenty of "bliss" and yet I have never said: "If I don't masturbate this morning, I will not fulfill my destiny." It just seems to happen. And that's why I'm able to do it so effortlessly. I give it no value. In fact, I give it a negative value – it might actually be hurting me (but that's for another book).

It's so unimportant in my life, that I can't stop doing it. That's why I'm so *successful* at it.

Eating pounds and pounds of fast food in one sitting is another bliss of mine, but do I ever say, "If I don't consume three Big Macs today my life will have no meaning? No, it just happens. No thought, no brain power required...it's like I'm some kind of *Zen master!* I just find myself magically in the drive-thru window every other day, ordering and then devouring massive, stuffed sacks of fried food in the parking lot. Within moments I'm at one with the eternal light – and that's even with a carload of gang bangers parked next to me.

"I am...and that's enough."
—Paris Hilton

To emphasize, the things that are truly blissful should have no value and require almost no thought. Here are three simple steps...

TRIUMPHANT ARTIST FACTS:

› Andy Warhol thought so little of his art that he painted soup cans

› Paul McCartney was not even concious when he wrote "Yesterday." He dreamt it.

› Robert Downey, Jr. won the Golden Globe for best actor despite being in and out of rehab more times than he slept in other people's houses.

Chapter 5: Creativity

Recite your mantra of destruction

The pathway to full creative realization rests with the utterance of a few simple words each morning to start your day:

Sit on the edge of your bed, play light music, (no whale or dolphin sounds, please). Take a few deep breaths, gently exhale and say:

My "Creative Life Pursuit" of _____
FILL IN THE BLANK
is less important than:

Switching from the Today Show *to* Good Morning America

Checking my tire pressure

Knowing the latest on what happened to that missing girl in Aruba

Renting "Bridget Jones Diary 2"

Playing online poker in trial mode for no money

Trying to remember who won the Super Bowl last year

Figuring out if the caps from ketchup bottles go into the recycling bin

Other: _____
FILL IN THE BLANK

National Lampoon *HELP!*

Rip down all your inspirational posters

No one needs the physical manifestation of your delusions of grandeur staring you in your face. If you're an actor, and you've got Jack Nicholson on your wall, that's not inspiration, that's a Times Square billboard with 5,000 lightbulbs flashing:

You have a 1-in-100 million chance to reach a Jack Nicholson-kind-of-greatness. You don't need to be reminded of this every day.

The remedy: Think of the most untalented people you know and plaster their pictures on your walls. If you're an actor, Ben Affleck will do. A musician or singer, Sanjaya Malakar. If you're a writer, a photo of me. A cartoonist, the guy who draws the "Love is" comics. If you're looking for an all-in-one that cov-

> *"I can care less every time I take the stage. It's getting off alive that worries me."*
> — *Kim Jong-il*
> *President, North Korea*

ers just about everything – a jumbo poster of Kato Kaelin will fit the bill.

These images will take the pressure off. You'll know that even when performing at the absolute lowest possible talent level you can still become a star. Now that's inspiration!

No pressure, no importance = sublime bliss.

Ohmmmmm!

Burn your self-help books

Go ahead, call me a fucking Nazi. Yes, I'm advocating the burning of books. But in a good way.

> *"A man's reach shall never exceed my nipples."*
> —Anna Nicole Smith

Every frustrated creative has "the shelf." It starts innocently enough. A few motivational books of the Deepak Chopra, Tony Robbins or perhaps even of the old school Andrew Carnegie variety. When you can't muster the energy to leave your bedroom before two in the afternoon, you start skimming the cognitive therapy books for snippets of information that will reprogram the way you react to your own negative thoughts, at least enough to get your fat ass out of the sack.

OK, so you tried that and it sorta worked. At least you're *ambulatory,* but your goal is be creative, so you begin to head toward the spiritual – the bridge book is usually "The Artist's Way." Once again, the results are limited, but you did manage to perform a one man show at an empty coffee house for a single night. You're on your way! Next up, "The Power of Now," which is sort of a portal leading you to read every book on Zen Buddhism.

Amazingly, after devouring twelve books on how to just "be in the moment," you're finally cast in your first play, and it's a paying gig at that! But you're so committed to being "aware of the present" that you are unable to remember the lines that you learned last week, and you begin to speak in tongues during the tech rehearsal.

> *"Your creative passion is to be cherished, nurtured, and revered.*
> *— The San Diego Chicken*

You're *fired*.

You get so depressed that you become the self-help equivalent of a skid row junkie. You're mainlining books on the Kabbalah and every single volume of L.Ron Hubbard's *Dianetics* series. Finally, you hit rock bottom – the Tony Alamo Ministry pamphlets.

It's been a long haul, and what do you have to show for it? A half written screenplay, a music demo with no background vocals, and a brief stint as Tevye in a production of "Fiddler on the Roof" at the local Jewish Center.

Look, you don't need these books around. You don't need to be reminded of all your failed attempts at self improvement. But more importantly, the presence of these books places unnecessary importance onto your creative passion.

So you must burn them!

Replace them all with trashy sex novels and biographies of obscure, mediocre talents that somehow rose to fame and prominence. I recommend MC Hammer's book, *I Can't Touch This*. Others can be found in the discount bin at Borders.

National Lampoon *HELP!*

Revelation # 2: Make Your Creative Pursuit a Part of Your Existing Bliss

You don't need help to pursue your dreams, you need a fucking doughnut.

"There's no better feeling than taking the stage with a cigarette in one hand and a martini in the other and belting out "That's Amore."
— John Lennon

When I dream, I'm eating doughnuts. So eat 'em. Pick up a dozen doughnuts and place them near your workspace. If you're a writer, after each paragraph written, you get to eat a doughnut. When a page is completed, masturbate. Tie them together, make them one... a Pavlovian circle jerk.

You must blur the lines between real and perceived bliss.

Don't wait to sell a script, a song, a painting to receive ecstasy. Reward yourself *now* with the very

Chapter 5: Creativity

> *"Being an artist requires nothing more than a fifth of Scotch and a bottle of 'ludes.*
> — Norman Rockwell

thing that gives you instant pleasure. After a while, you'll connect the pleasure of overeating and sexual self-satisfaction with your creative endeavor. In a couple of weeks you'll begin to crave writing music or painting as much as flipping through the new issue of *Maxim*. You'll salivate when you come up with your next idea, you'll *sport wood* at the thought of going to your next audition.

You can do it! Now call up Domino's and get to work!

Revelation # 3: Drugs and Alcohol are Keys to Success

It seems to me that nearly every major creative artist was or is a drug addict, an alcoholic or both. Lenny Bruce, John Lennon, Richard Pryor, Kurt Cobain, Edgar Alan Poe, Lindsay Lohan – the list is endless.

So, if almost every fully-realized creative is a substance abuser, it would only be logical to assume that the way to flourish at your creative pursuit is to get on the pipe as well. But I know what you're thinking...

"I don't want to die!!!"

That's fair. No one does. And it's unfortunate that there's nobody around to help us navigate through these deadly substances while we concentrate on developing our art.

Well, almost nobody. That guy with the pay-as-you-go cellphone hanging around outside the strip club who only answers to Bro or Homey is a veritable Wikipedia of substance abuse knowledge. For most creative dreamers, our dealer is the only *real* art teacher we'll ever know in the competitive world of art.

But it's a shame that you can only garner this information from street hustlers. To my knowledge, no legitimate Drama, Communications, or Music Department in the country offers courses in managing personal substance abuse. But with the artist mortality rate higher than that of the Shi'ite militia, this situation is certainly bound to change.

> *"At this stage of my life, I know of no other way to get publicity other than to enter rehab or stage my own fake death yet again."*
> — Sinbad

Ideally, the fine arts instructor of tomorrow will be a perfect blend of pharmacist and teacher – more akin to a Thirteenth Century alchemist than to a modern college professor. For the purposes of this book, I'll don the robe and assume that role. And I'll just assume you already know how to acquire the hard stuff and are probably already a stoner, heroin addict, glue sniffer, or worse. If so, I can suggest ways for you to turn that "monkey on your back" into your own private muse.

THESE ARE ONLY SUGGESTIONS. I AM NOT A DOCTOR, BIOLOGIST, SCIENTIST, PHARMACIST, PSYCHIATRIST OR THORACIC SURGEON. DO NOT ATTEMPT ILLEGAL DRUG USE OR ABUSIVE ALCOHOL CONSUMPTION WITHOUT THE KNOWLEDGE THAT YOUR LIFE WILL BE A NEVER-ENDING HELL ON EARTH.

Okay, with that out of the way, let's start reviewing your options. The following are two sample college courses that any credible drama department should add to its curriculum.

Although we'll use acting as an example, these valuable lessons may be applied to any art form...

Chapter 5: Creativity

NATIONAL LAMPOON

SCHOOL OF DRAMA

Course Schedule

DRAMA 101
ILLICIT DRUG TAKING FOR THE STAGE

Introduction to the proper use of pharmaceuticals for the enhancement of stage performance

Any acting student must be able to sense the right amount of drugs & alcohol that he requires to soar during a Shakespearean performance without jeopardizing their vocal prowess and public reputation.

In this six month workshop for beginning students, the young actors will be asked to re-examine their work methods as they prepare for a career in the performing arts. Students' performances will be assessed in the following manner:

Case Study: The Budding Young Actor with a Vicodin Habit
If the actor begins to deliver the famous Hamlet soliloquy and suddenly we hear, "To be uhrrr nodda be." – no matter how well he's conveying the character's inner turmoil, the student must immediately cut back at least 250 milligrams on his Vicodin. But caution is advised. If the dosage is reduced too much, he risks losing the remarkable emotive quality of the performance and the dangerously exciting, out-of-control sword fight.

More adjustments may be necessary. To fine tune the performance, try taking a swig of Grey Goose one hour before the opening curtain, and two hours after the Vicodin kicks in. No more, no less.

But be prepared for variables. It's quite likely that the student has toked pot or hash sometime during the school day. If this is the case, the student must cut back at least two bong hits, and take one shot of tequila just before his stage entrance.

As we've seen, determining just the right combination of alcohol and pills for optimal performance is very difficult, even sobering. That's why these lessons should be learned in college, and not on the set of "Grey's Anatomy."

Chapter 5: Creativity   **87**

**DRAMA 102
PATHWAY TO STARDOM**

Examination of the artist's daily schedule and abuse methodologies as applied to the career path of a typical actor.

Sample: An Actor's Life

10AM: Utter dread of a new day
= standard 5 bong hits upon waking

2PM: Nervous about the upcoming night's performance
= 2 Vicodin taken

6PM: Feeling too jittery, scared fake beard will fall off
= 1 shot of Rum

7:30PM: Curtain opens, panic sets in
= emergency bong hit and swig of Tequila

Intermission: Beard fell off
= another Vicodin, washed down with Tequila

10PM: Great show, however, amped-up from performance
= 5 mixed drinks at cast party

2PM: Pass-out

Repeat daily schedule for 10 years until entering rehab.

Replace illegal drugs with therapist-prescribed psychotropics.

Use publicity of entering and reentering rehab to lengthen career an additional 10 years.

Repeat cycle until death

In Conclusion

A person's creative dreams never go away. They haunt him until his final breath and even then there's still one last gasp to pitch the hospice nurse an idea about a dying man who never lived his dreams. But don't let your eptiath be your most seen piece of work. You've got something to offer this world. Now get out there and remember:

Nothing is less important than the importance of your art.

Chapter 6
Stress Management

In This Chapter...

✔ To be homeless is to be stressless

✔ Live like it's 1985!

✔ A new calendar for the crazed modern man.

Choosing A New Life Paradigm

We are a society out of control, whirling through space and time with no direction, no purpose, and completely overloaded. I don't know anybody who's not out of their fucking minds. There's just too much enticing stuff, it's too easy to access it, and not nearly enough time to do anything with it.

And our society has stripped a way the only two coping mechanisms we have: drinking and smoking. Sure everything on the walls had a faint yellow tint on it but people were at least *calm* back then, dammit! Even your hellish commute was filled with a blissful, hypnotic, road induced coma without a single cell phone interruption from your bipolar girlfriend.

Now everybody is even more stressed out and instead of harmless vices all we have to sooth our shattered nerves is a sheet of bubble wrap to pop and those staple remover claws to self-mutilate ourselves with.

Are we kidding? Do we really think we can manage stress without causing even more stress?

It's about as hopeless as figuring out what desk to hide under when the next slighted employee goes on a shotgun rampage.

Stress Management

That's gotta be the granddaddy of insane oxymorons. No amount of management or Tony Robbins motivational seminars is going to give hope to that pathetic junior exec quivering in the corner cubicle with a chocolate-latte-tsunami building momentum in his violently shaking coffee mug.

> "I have a BlackBerry in one hand, a cell phone in the other, and — Jesus Fucking Christ! — I still can't get anything accomplished!"
> — Condoleeza Rice
> US Secretary of State

When it comes to dealing with stress, one thing is certain. Freedom from stress can only be achieved through action. *Bold* action. *Desperate* action. Even *stupid* action. Trust me, I've actually been hospitalized for stress and have spent countless hours of company time considering all the angles on how to beat it.

Here are just a few of the stressless lifestyle choices I recommend:

Become a Homeless Person

It's the perfect lifestyle choice for a stress-free existence. They've accepted a life of nothing, like trappist monks with great hair (and a greater tolerance for head lice). They don't have to answer their instant messaging or emails, or call people back on their cell. They don't have to send endless birthday, anniversary, get well, thank you, hip-cool-esoteric greeting cards to friends & relatives.

"My life was much better when I lived in my car."
— KFed

When you're homeless, the only other person you have to deal with is your other self – you know, the one across the street screaming wildly while dropping a deuce in front of your ex-wife's gleaming downtown office building.

Your whole life is completely manageable as a homeless person. Everything you need fits nicely into a three-and-a-half wheel Ralph's shopping cart. Add a little cardboard paneling, squint your eyes, and your ride looks a lot like one of those pimped-out Woody wagons in the Frankie and Annette Beach Blanket movies. And like Moondoggie, you're living the ideal beach bum life, only without the beach. No stress. No money. No worries. No teeth.

Cowabunga!

Live like the Amish

Live *like* the Amish, but not *among* them.

Follow their teachings about austerity and all that shit, but ignore the one about 1759 being the year when all of man's earthly necessities were provided by God. I mean, really. Getting around Intercourse, PA in a horse & buggy is at least as stressful as any rush hour commute on the 405 in your fishtailing Corolla. After sundown on the Sabbath, you're still gonna get drunk and chase poontang till 3 AM, so the last thing you need is some ancient beast of burden putting a hitch in your giddyup.

> *"Taking a vow of silence is easy, not IM-ing is hard"*
> — *Trappist Monk Bernardo Esteva*

Besides, the year 1759 was *not* when God stopped handing us all the crap we needed to sustain our mortal existence. It was 1985. By 1985, we had every technological necessity — but nothing quite good enough to form a long lasting addiction to it and cause us needless stress. Video games were good, but there's only so far you can go with *Donkey Kong* and

Chapter 6: Stress Management

Ms. Pac Man. We had those tiny Macintosh computers with 4 MB of RAM and they worked OK, but how long could you really stare at a Lotus 1-2-3 on a four inch monochrome screen anyway?

Back in 1985, we basically had everything and nothing. And like the Amish, life was simple. Even our pop icons looked kinda Amish. Remember Boy George? What about C. Everett Coop?

And it wasn't that long ago. You can practically *drive* there!

Get back to 1985

Everything's possible if you want it bad enough.

Following are simple steps you can use to return to your own stress-free Pennsylvania Dutch lifestyle – circa 1985.

> *"I'd do anything to get back to 1985 including driving a DeLorean filled with stolen plutonium."*
> *— Downtown Julie Brown*

How to Time Travel to 1985:

1. **Call your cable or satellite company and tell them you'll be dropping everything except TV Land.**

   A couple of episodes of "The Cosby Show" and "Family Ties" and you'll be able to wean yourself off Xanax and Klonopin in no time.

2. **Smash your cell phone and replace it with a set of Transformers Walkie Talkies.**

   No charges, no weekend plans, no family rates, no rollover minutes, no favorite five, no roaming charges. Just uninterrupted, free communication with your best friend as long as he stays within a 100 feet of you, and your mother's not using her blow dryer. Can you hear me now?

3. **Rip out your car's navigation system and replace it with leaning out your window and asking a total stranger for directions.**

   Chances are the directions will be wrong but at least you would have made contact with the outside world. Plus, you'll be able to tell people a real excuse why you're late – "I got lost." Instead of just being a jackass and making something up that no one living in the 21st Century would ever believe.

4. **No more Internet, get a Rubiks Cube**

   It will eat up the same amount of time and you'll become equally obsessed, but at least you won't fill your mind with deviant sexual fetishes that should have stayed within the domain of perverts, sadists, and pedophiles.

5. **Exchange your Wii for a ColecoVision**

   For once, you'll sleep easy. No more night terrors after a particularly intense game of "Call of Duty 3". Instead, you'll enjoy the relatively stress-free play of "Smurfs: Rescue in Gargamel's Castle." Sweet!

6. **Shitcan your HD DVR and replace it with a Sony Betamax.**

   I know. I know. Your local Blockbuster's selection of Beta format videotapes occupies less than half the shelf space of the Rocky Balboa clearance display, but still, you have to ask yourself this question: Is there really anything left to watch after Police Academy IV?

Chapter 6: Stress Management **97**

Create A New Calendar Made For Today's World

Human beings are not wired to handle the endless tasks a single day demands. We come from a cave! And it was just 6000 years ago! Maybe we had three things on the cave wall to-do list for the entire year:

1. *Get food.*
2. *Eat food.*
3. *Rape.*

That was it! And although human civilization has evolved, any anthropologist will tell you that our brains have not. We are still essentially the same guys – *cave men.*

> *"There's never enough time to do what needs to be done"*
> — **Adolph Hitler**

When people say to you, "I can't right now. I don't have the bandwidth" – *THEY DON'T HAVE THE BANDWIDTH!* There's no creating a new "Priority Action Matrix," no Tai Chi, no "slowly repeating a calm word," no adjustment of your "Hostility Log," no "smelling lavender" – you're done! There is no stress management. The RAM is full, with only room for one more task: to rip your clothes off and run down the street naked screaming, "Someone kill me! Please someone just kill me!"

We are not meant to use our brains in the ways that we are made to use them today.

And here's why:

National Lampoon HELP!

We don't have enough time in a day to do everything!

Lets take a look at the most basic activities & tasks of a typical day:

- *8 hours sleep*

- *3 hours sitting at the coffee house pondering life*

- *1 hour masturbating*

- *2 hour post masturbation nap*

- 3 hours eating

- *4 hours watching TV*

- *4 hours on the internet*

- *1 hour going to the bathroom*

Now that's just a normal day and that's like 26 hours. And we haven't even included any of the stressful stuff of a normal day.

You must add the following:

- *3 hour commute to work*

- *8 hour work day*

- *3 hours to shop for your girlfriend's Valentine Day gift*

- *1 hour conversation with DMV to learn how to fight your traffic ticket*

- *3 hour conversation with Dell Computer in India to learn why your new laptop takes 10 minutes to boot up*

- *1 hour tracking the lost UPS package you sent to your Dad for his 65th birthday*

- *72 hours responding to the urgent email from your bank that your identity has been stolen and you need to change all your accounts immediately*

- *2 hour trip to the vet because your dog is projectile vomiting while exploding out of its ass. It's determined that she ate the chocolate valentine you were going to give your girlfriend*

- *3 hours to replace Valentine's Day gift*

That adds up to 96 hours for 1 day plus the 26 hours for the normal day activities.

That equals:

122 hours that is needed to accomplish a typical day!

And how can you cut any of this out? You can't! There's simply no where to cut!

There's only one solution:

National Lampoon **HELP!**

Change what a day is!

Yes, redefine it. Since a real day requires 122 hours, make this the new day:

Decide that each day is 122 hours!

> "Even a good man can not accomplish all that needs to be done in 24 hours without torturing a lot of people."
> — Jack Bauer

Imagine how great this would be — only one hellish commute in the equivalent of five days! And it can be done; they instituted a new Daylight Savings Time. Why not go all the way and redefine a day, even a week, or a month. Redo the whole calendar to adjust to our maddening lives.

Remarkably, we still use a calendar based on archaic notions of sun gods, planetary worship and the movement of the stars. It's insanity to allow these ancient pagan rituals to dictate our lives.

I don't know about you, but I haven't seen a star outside my house in 15 years – I have to take a leap of faith that they're still up there.

I propose a new calendar, still based on the movement of the stars, but the stars our civilization can actually *see:* Paris Hilton, Brittany Spears, Halle Berry, Lindsay Lohan, etc.

This new 122-hour day-based calendar will be founded on a proven scientific cycle much more precise than any celestial body moving across the sky:

Chapter 6: Stress Management

The Skank Cycle — aka "The Star Meltdown."

Every 5 days, an American female star humiliates themselves in a delicious drug and alcohol induced public meltdown. It is guaranteed and it is science. No longer will this precise rhythm of the stars just serve the interests of the National Enquirer and the Promises rehab facility. It will now become the foundation for how we measure the passage of time.

The New American Star Calendar

Based on the Skank Cycle.™

The NASMC is designed to make our lives flow effortlessly as we engage in a frantic world. The calendar consists of two parts: One "day" is 122 hours (the Skank Cycle) and one "month" is five days. That's it. There are no weeks. This should give everybody plenty of time to accomplish what needs to get done without feeling even a tinge of pressure.

"I think we should change the calendar. Maybe I can show more ass next year?"
— Pamela Anderson

The following spread illustrates how this revolutionary new calendar could work.

National Lampoon *HELP!*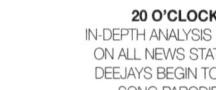

0 O'CLOCK
CELEBRITY SKANK SCANDAL APPEARS AS "BREAKING NEWS" ON CNN'S TICKER.

20 O'CLOCK
IN-DEPTH ANALYSIS BEGINS ON ALL NEWS STATIONS. DEEJAYS BEGIN TO PLAY SONG PARODIES.

40 O'CLOCK
INTERNET ANIMATION USING MUG AND/OR BEAVER SHOTS REACH 25 MILLION HITS AT NATIONALLAMPOON.COM

60 O'CLOCK
THE TEARFUL, YET DEFIANT CELEBRITY SKANK VOWS TO GET BETTER IN REHAB. ENTERS $5,000/DAY 'WELLNESS CENTER' IN BEVERLY HILLS.

START OF THE SKANK CYCLE

Janu

| **1** | Nicole Richie arrested for a DUI | **2** | Britney Spears passes out at a nightclub | **3** | Lindsay Lohan enters re |

Chapter 6: Stress Management   **103**

80 O'CLOCK
CELEBRITY SKANK CHECKS OUT OF REHAB TO ATTEND BITCHIN' PARTY WITH FORMER MOTLEY CRUE MEMBER AND/OR NEW LESBIAN FRIEND.

100 O'CLOCK
MEDIA SCRUTINY PEAKS WITH NANCY GRACE CALLING FOR PUBLIC CRUCIFIXION OF CELEBRITY SKANK. CONSERVATIVE PUNDITS DECRY THE STATE OF AMERICA'S YOUTH.

122 O'CLOCK
CELEBRITY SKANK APPEARS WITH OPRAH AND/OR DR. PHIL TO BLAME HER PARENTS. IN THE CASE OF CELEBRITY SKANK'S DEATH, THE SKANK IS BURIED.
CYCLE BEGINS AGAIN.

END OF THE SKANK CYCLE

| 4 | Anna Nicole Smith dies | 5 | Britney Spears shaves her head |

In Conclusion

Managing stress is not manageable. Don't be fooled by all the new age gurus who claim you can manage your time. This is insane! How would you ever find the time to manage your time? You can't! It is an unrealistic utopian concept that only can be realized through the creation of new paradigms that completely redefine our lives.

So do it. Pick one of the choices above. Take that one massive leap into the abyss and I assure you that the only stress you'll ever have is trying to decide whether you should go *into* the McDonalds or just use the Drive Thru.

Chapter 7
Love & Relationships

In This Chapter...

✔ Men can't compete with women

✔ Take our lives, please!

✔ Her ignorance is bliss

Having it All by Letting Her Think She Has it All

The New Woman wants to be a Man. It's true. No matter how misogynistic it might sound, women want to wear the Dockers in our society. They want to play all our sports: There are women Football leagues, Rugby leagues. More and more, they are becoming our bosses – there are women executives in nearly every fortune 500 company. They even serve gallantly in the military. My God, they want to be President and *will* be!

Well that's great and congratulations and all that. But did anybody ever ask: What the hell happens to us guys? We now have to compete with them. It was bad enough competing with other guys but now with women, too?!

"A man needs a Yin to his Yang. There just can't be two Yangs. If I want a guy, I'll go all the way and get a guy."
— Pat Robertson

Our natural inclination is to help women by *not* competing with them. Most men will still hold a door open for a woman. They will still let them take better seats in a restaurant. How can we go in for the competitive kill when our nature says we should lend them a hand? We can't, so we're *fucked*.

And when you toss-in a woman's ability to shrewdly use her sexuality to get what she wants from a man – only for us dumb apes to misread the signals and end up with a Sexual Harassment Lawsuit – we can't compete.

But if somehow we do manage to defeat them in the workplace, we'll ultimately face a landmark Gender Bias Lawsuit that will destroy our careers and the companies we works for.

It gets worse. What used to define us as men, our brute strength, has been rendered completely useless. There's a petite-sized gizmo for every task that used to require a man's muscle. Electric can openers, power drills, and dildos – they don't even need our *dicks* anymore.

It's over. Don't you see? We can't win. Feminism was once a cute little hippie chick obsession but no

longer. The gals have won and won big. Women will soon rule the world. But that's the bad news!

The good news is: *we lost.*

Let them work 12 hour days and bring home the bacon and a nasty alcohol problem. Let them develop a 2 pack a day Merit Lights habit and a peculiar, stress-related rectal itch. Let their gender die 7 years earlier than ours. Let 'em have the whole enchilada. Go for it ladies!

Hell, they're pretty good at it anyway. I'm not sure about football, but running companies and stuff, well sure, why the hell not.

Take Our Lives...Please!

Hallelujah! Praise Jesus! The Feminist Revolution has opened an amazing window of opportunity that is now available to all men.

We get to have their old lives. It's a guy paradise!

The new man is a 1950's woman

It's wide open and there for the taking. No one wants it. And we just have to grab it. Women don't want it - they're too busy "proving themselves" – and it hasn't even occurred yet to guys that it's even a remotely viable option.

But it is. And by God it seems almost too, too good to be true...

- **NO** *staying at the office until 11 PM*
- **NO** *grueling 5 MPH commutes!*
- **NO** *asshole bosses to beg for raises!*
- **NO** *degrading power plays!*
- **NO** *writing reports that no one reads!*
- **NO** *endless, butt-numbing meetings!*
- **NO** *meaningless water cooler chit-chat!*

We get to stay home and do our thing. It's awesome: Poker games, sports conversations, afternoon rendezvous' with a series of mistresses and whores, while they're at office busting their sorry ass. Sure, there's some house work and some minor child rearing (although we'll let day care handle most of that), but hey, it's a small price to pay to hang out and do whatever the hell we want.

"I remember being a kid, coming home from school and seeing my mother in the kitchen sitting around, laughing with her friends, drinking coffee. I swore then that was the life I wanted."
— *Matt Lauer*

We'll gladly stay at home and eat Breyers and watch our favorite shows. And the great thing about it is that when enough men finally do this, the whole afternoon TV schedule will change. No more soap operas or Oprahs, it will be *all* sports *all*

Chapter 7: Love & Relationships

> "I'd change fifty diapers and do twelve loads of laundry in exchange for not having to go to work tomorrow."
> — Robert Gates, US Secretary of Defense

afternoon, with action shows, and *Family Guy* reruns in the off-season.

Within a couple of years, the NFL will broadcast every day of the week during the afternoon hours. No more waiting for Sunday afternoon (what's that about anyway, that should be a family day!) or waiting for Monday night football when you're completely spent from work. You see, it all makes sense.

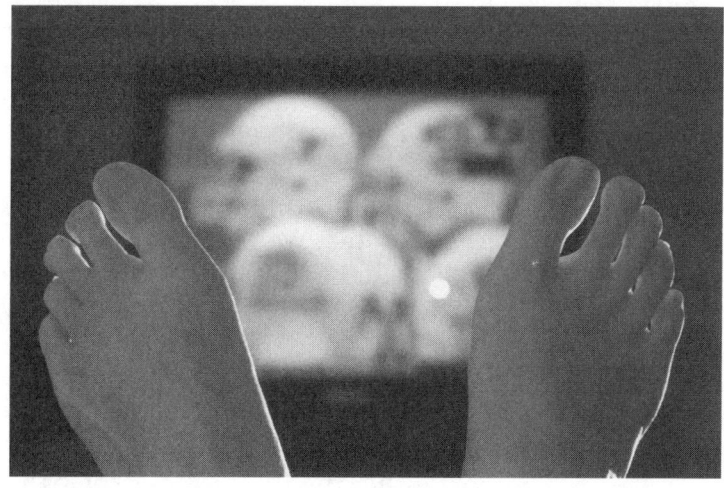

And once Madison Avenue realizes that we now buy all the crap for the home, advertisers will do anything to reach us.

They already use hot babes to sell us beer, cars, and boats, but wait until Proctor & Gamble gears up to sell us Tide, Lemon Pledge, and Swiffers. Hot babes wil arrive at your door with free samples and a complimentary lap dance. Guys, this can be our world. Every commercial on TV will have hot babes selling us dishwashing liquid and shampoo.

It will be glorious!

And we get to bitch and bitch and bitch all day with each other instead of holding it in our whole lives and dying prematurely from a heart attack at the Sizzler All-You-Can-Eat Rib Buffet.

This is the fountain of youth. We'll look great! No stress! Our hair will be cut once a week, maybe take in a massage. What could be better?

> "I don't know, I've been a woman my whole life and it's not so much better."
> — *John Edwards, Presidential Candidate*

There will be no more arguments with our ladies. We'll let them win everything. Let 'em have it. And why not? We got to play *Grand Theft Auto III* until 9 PM with Larry (the now *retired* Cable Guy) and that was after taking-in a Cubs double header .

We'll be finally free to truly be guys but more importantly, true to our inner selves.

Free to be the men we were meant to be, swollen masses of sugar, fat, farts, and beer with absolutely no guilt or pressure to behave like the soulless, hate-

Chapter 7: Love & Relationships

filled Yuppies we once were. At long last, we can live our lives with *personal integrity*.

We are so much better suited to be in the old woman's role than women ever were. We are the original "couch potatoes." The term was coined for us, not them. And now it can be our God given right. Our manifest destiny.

And it's a great time to do it – it's 2007. We don't have to make soap, or wash clothes by hand. It's all done for us now!

Can it get any better?

Hell no, but women are notoriously fickle and could change their minds about this "new world order" any minute…so now's the time *seal the deal*.

Take this Oath!

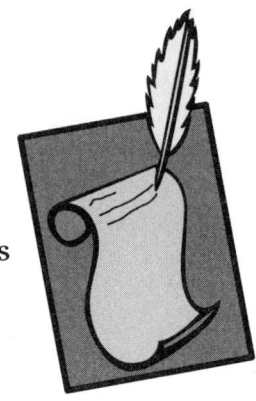

If you're lucky enough to find yourself in a committed relationship with a woman that has embraced her masculine self, you must sign, date, and present the following oath to her immediately. And be sure to have it notarized!

You'll be amazed at how many women will find this approach refreshing, thoughtful and even sweet. They'll feel validated as a "modern woman" and you can go back to surfing for porn.

I'd say that's a win-win.

Chapter 7: Love & Relationships

TO MY LIFE PARTNER AND SOULMATE:

I DO SOLEMNLY SWEAR TO RELINQUISH MY ANCIENT RIGHTS AS A MAN TO "GO OUT AND CONQUER THE WORLD."

I AM CONTENT TO ALLOW YOU, AS THE DOMINANT GENDER, TO LEAD ME AND WHAT'S LEFT OF MY DYING CIVILIZATION INTO THE NEXT MILLENIUM.

I HAVE NO ASPIRATIONS OTHER THAN TO DO SOME LIGHT HOUSEWORK AND SOME DEGREE OF CHILD REARING (MOSTLY DRIVING, PLAYING HORSIE & PICKING 'EM UP FROM DAYCARE).

IF A DISAGREEMENT SHALL OCCUR BETWEEN US DURING OUR RELATIONSHIP, I WILL SUBMIT TO YOUR SUPERIOR WISDOM AND JUDGEMENT.

I FREELY ACCEPT, AND YOU HEREBY ACKNOWLEDGE, THAT IT IS YOUR RESPONSIBILITY AS A MODERN WOMAN TO PROVIDE FOR THE FAMILY.

I ENTER INTO THIS OATH BEING OF SOUND MIND AND FREE WILL ON THIS DATE,

THE _____ OF _____, 20____

SIGNATURE: _____

Finding Your Ideal Woman-Man

In order to create this fantastic Guy-Lifestyle you must find your very own woman-man.

Of course New York and LA are overrun with these aggressive women. If you are so blessed geographically, finding one should be as easy as spotting any human being walking with a pair of tits. However, if you happen to live outside the big city, here are some clues to help you identify your future wife and provider.

The Signals:

- ✔ Any woman driving a Hummer

- ✔ Any woman that's fanatic about an NFL team

- ✔ Any woman in a supervisory role in a high-rise business tower

- ✔ Any woman that arrives five minutes early to Friday Night Happy Hour

- ✔ Any woman that never puts on a dress unless it's to pick up an award for her professional achievements

- ✔ Any woman who arrives home at 8:30 PM on a Wednesday night, then gets out of her car with a briefcase and a KFC bucket while still making business calls on her cell.

Chapter 7: Love & Relationships   **117**

SOME WOMEN HAVE GONE TOO FAR AS GUYS, AND THEY ARE NOW FULL-ON LESBIANS. IT'S IMPORTANT THAT YOU GET THEM JUST BEFORE THEY TURN. FOR INSTANCE: PICKING UP A WOMAN AT A WNBA GAME...YOU'RE TOO LATE. NFL GAME? JUST RIGHT.

Now if you can't seem to find someone or you happen to live in the bible belt, you might want to consider an alternative. These days most of the really great women are actually rich gay guys and tall, exotic transsexuals. So if you're open-minded, don't overlook this option. It's worth noting that genetic males are generally pretty easy to hook up with... or so I've *heard*.

How Do I Maintain this Crazy Charade?

If you are to pull this off, you must be their cheerleader. Don't worry, you won't have to prance around in a Laker Girls outfit, but you will have to make them feel that someone cares about their effort and sacrifice. You are that person.

And relax...this requires almost no effort.

At most, it is a single five minute phone call every other day at 3 PM. That's it. They will barely have time to talk to you – which is great because it's another Tuesday double-header at Wrigley and you're running late to the first inning.

In addition, when they come home, just simply ask, "How was your day Dear?" That's it. There should be no emotion attached – only spoken as rote.

It's really that simple.

There might be the occasional foot massage, but you can incorporate that into your perfunctory sex act later in the evening.

Our little guy secret...

Of course you will never let on that we don't actually do anything during the day. Always make it sound like housework is the hardest job in the world.

Now, in order to sustain this myth, you'll have to voice your complaints in measured doses so as not to jeopardize your hard-won Shangri-La. You can't allow them to get any ideas about quitting their jobs and *reversing* the situation.

COMPLAIN TOO MUCH AND THEY'LL LEAVE YOU. THEN IT'S BACK TO HARD TIME AS A SEASONAL TAX PREPARER AT H&R BLOCK – AND THE GIG IS UP.

Chapter 7: Love & Relationships 119

Here are some sample complaint lines. Use them sparingly to project the illusion of productivity:

- "It's so damn hard, with all this laundry all the time and would you look at all the dishes!"

- "I had to go to the Dry Cleaners and then do a big grocery shopping – in one day. I'm sorry if I didn't make it to the bank too, shoot me!"

- "You think you have it bad? I had to wait *two hours* for the lady plumber today and I missed my hairstyling appointment!"

- "I know your day was hard, dear, but do you think I have it easy? I had to pay all the bills and pick up *your* daughter from day care... I couldn't leave the house before 11!"

Just utter those nuggets now and then, and you'll scare them back to work.

Ignorance is bliss!

Never share with your woman the endless hours of recreation that this heavenly new lifestyle offers.

This includes the following:

- ✔ Blowing up fireworks on Martin Luther King day.

- ✔ A visit to the Arena Football League's talent scout combine

- ✔ a day trip to the Coyote Valley Shodakai Casino to play slots, place your sports bets for the month and watch a comped showing of the Amazing Jonathon's superb magic act

- ✔ A gentlemen's game of lawn darts

- ✔ Baseball fantasy day camp

- ✔ Lighting your farts

- ✔ Googling your name

- ✔ A brewery tour of the local Budweiser plant

They must never learn of our secret ecstasy!

In Conclusion

Women embracing their masculine side is the greatest single event that has ever happened to men in the past five thousand years. The sooner you accept this new gender switch, the sooner you can begin your amazing new life. Don't waste any more time, Guy Shangri-La awaits.

Chapter 8

Mental Health

In This Chapter...

✔ Stare at the pictures – your life is good!

✔ That gut of yours is not from starvation

✔ No one's moving to Buffalo

Conquering Depression

If the wisdom in this book is applied, depression will be a rare event, only reserved for freak days, like when they end the Third Pounder promotion at McDonalds or when the engine finally seizes on your decade-old Jag. These blips can momentarily throw you off your path to the fulfillment of nothing and send you spiraling into a sea of darkness. Typically these dark moods will pass in a few hours and after consuming an entire pint of Ben & Jerry's Mocha Munch in front of the TV.

"If I had only known how tired I would feel at 50, I would have killed myself sooner."
— *Hunter S. Thompson*

But if you are still depressed three days later, drastic action must be taken.

If you want to get over your funk without meds or without babbling on about it for five years to a psychologist who earned her degree from University of Phoenix, or even worse, receive a series of colonics from the holistic healer down the street only to find out it's a front for Scientology – here's what you do...

"Knock It The Fuck Off!!!!"

No one is coming for you, you've got food and shelter, and you can leave that shelter whenever you want for a mad dash to In & Out Burger. In your *car*.

Do you have any idea how good you have it?

You could have been born in Hungary in the Thirteenth century and been brutally ass-raped and quartered by Mongol hordes. If somehow you managed to survive that shit, don't worry, the Black Plague was just around the corner, followed by the Spanish Inquisition, the Return of the Black Plague, the 100 Years War, the Civil War, WWII, etc.

"When the darkness creeps in, I don't fight it, I acknowledge it and surrender to it, and then polish off a box of Entemann's donuts."
— *Jack LaLanne*

But you were born in America in the second half of the 20th century. Even if your home is in a white trash Kentucky trailer, modern plumbing alone means you live better than King Henry VIII. When's the last time you used a chamber pot?

Look, by the time this book comes out, it's likely that you live in the third greatest country in the world (seems like we drop down a notch every six months), but dammit, third place is still pretty good.

And you're *depressed?*

Maybe you need a reminder, a brush-up of sorts, of just how good you really have it.

Chapter 8: Mental Health **127**

NATIONAL LAMPOON

HORRIFYING IMAGE

SHOCK TREATMENT THERAPY

Instructions:

1. Stare at the following horrifying images.

2. Let each one seep deeply into your subconscious.

3. Read the caption under each photo.

4. Repeat each caption to yourself 10 times while not breathing.

Chapter 8: Mental Health **129**

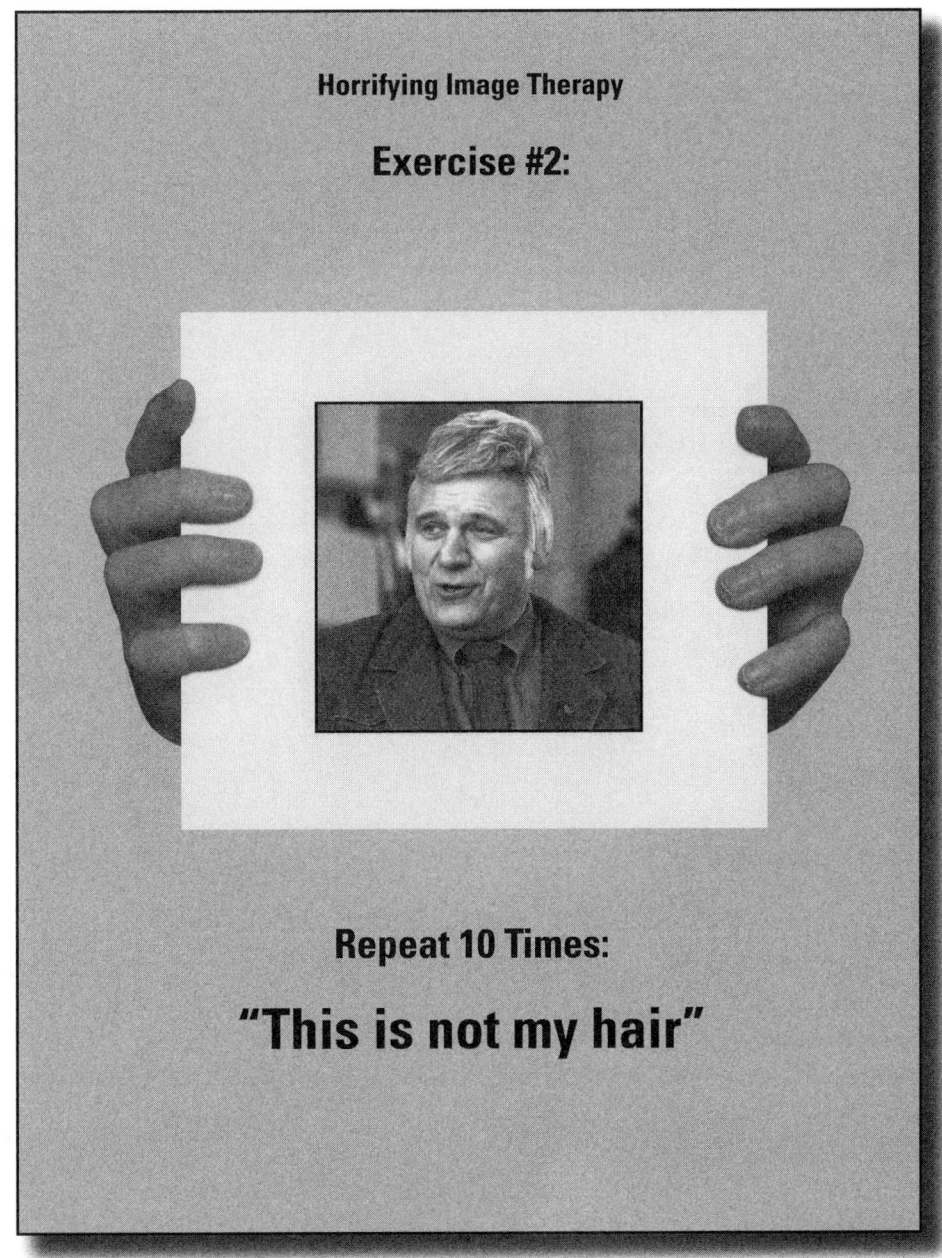

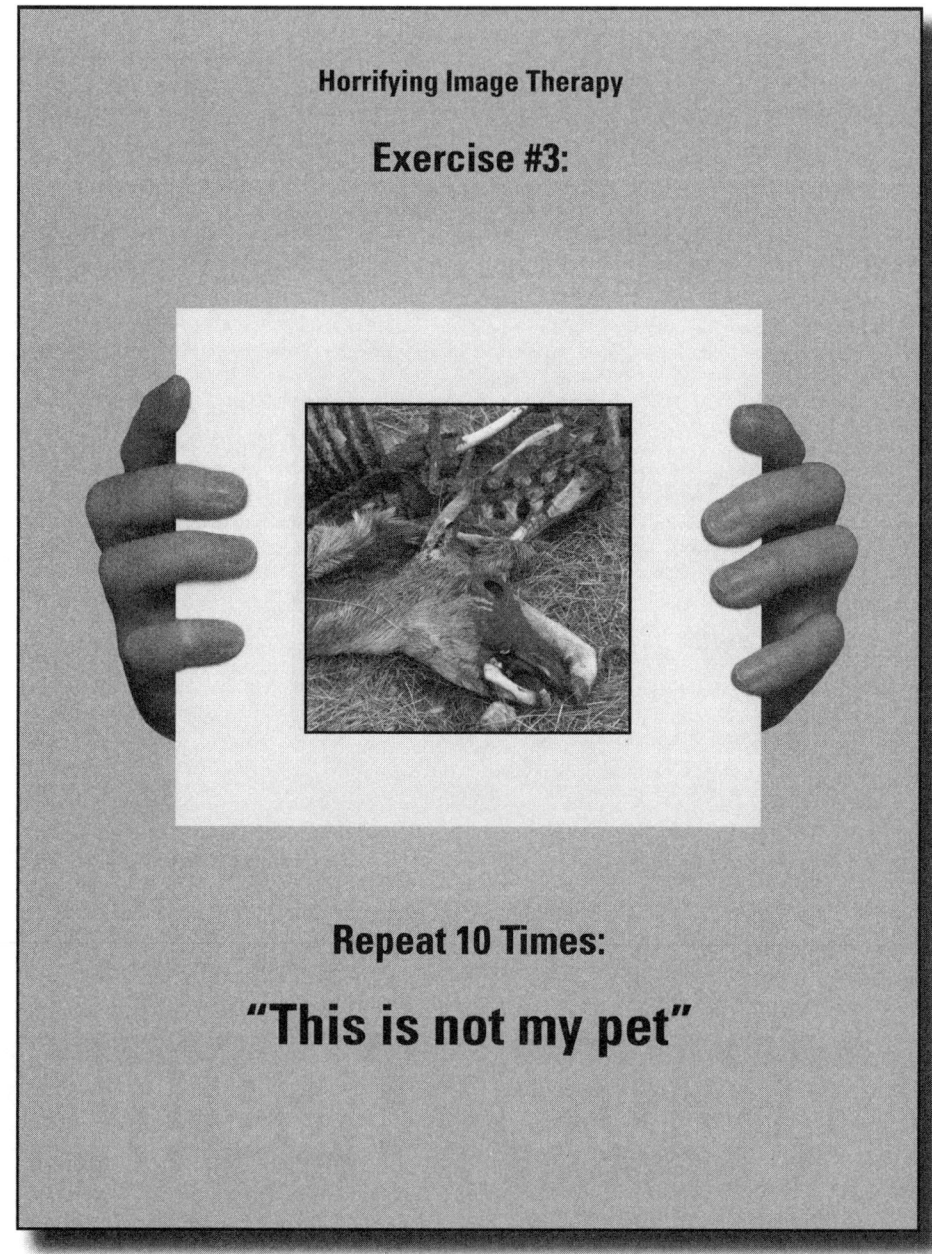

Chapter 8: Mental Health — 131

Horrifying Image Therapy

Exercise #4:

Repeat 10 Times:

"I am not this guy"

Get the picture?

OK, OK, so maybe these Horrifying Images are not as bad as some you've seen on the Internet. You know, like the ones from gag-a-maggot.com that you have bookmarked in your browser.

But humor me. Let's pretend that the pictures you've just seen are in fact *much more* horrible than my publisher will allow me to print in this book.

I mean really, *really* horrible.

So horrible, in fact, that you awake from your catatonic Red Bull and X-Box stupor to realize, at long last, just how privileged and indeed *spoiled fucking rotten* you are compared to the teeming mass of far less fortunate souls on this festering planet.

But still, you're anxious and depressed. Your "man tits" twitch for no reason. You're sick with fear, consumed by dread, and restless leg syndrome keeps you up till the wee hours. You're little more than a pulsating, bioluminescent sac of raw nerve endings.

And these disturbing questions remain…

Dr. Rubin's Nutcase Q&A

If you aren't convinced by now that your life is truly blessed and sprinkled with rose petals, then you are no doubt *really fucking nuts* and beyond any sort of professional help or therapy. Despite this grave prognosis, I'll make one last attempt to address your mental health issues and get you back on the road to wellness.

The following is a hypothetical Q&A between you and me. After reading this section, if you're still depressed, then just close the book and get away from me before I call security.

Q: *I guess my life isn't so bad, but the world can still blow up tomorrow in a nuclear holocaust, right? Doesn't that Iranian guy in the taupe Dickies jacket have a bomb?*

A: Now, what asshole would want to miss the end of the fucking world!

It beats watching it every week on *24*. At least you'll get to see the "live" feed and witness all of that Revelation and Second Coming stuff that Benny Hinn has been promising us for years.

Think about it. With all the tens of billions of people ever born since the dawn of man, *you get to be the last one out the door!* It just doesn't get any more special than that.

Q: *But what about global warming? Isn't that a slow, torturous death? And all those cute, cuddly polar bears...aren't they headed for extinction?*

A: Listen up. It's global *warming,* Not global *cooling* – now that would be a setback. What's the problem with warming? Every person I know either lives in Florida and California or wants to move there... why? Because it's warm! Really warm! Butt-crack warm!

The native Indian populations have always known this. Warm good. Cold bad. For god's sake, people are migrating to the desert in droves. Arizona and Nevada are booming! Do people in Arizona worry about global warming? No, they have red hot sun rays on their state flag! The place is a goddam wood-fired pizza oven and it's all sand to boot. How can it possibly get any worse than that? Except for the heat, the Southwestern US is nearly identical to the surface of Mars — there's no water and nothing can live there. And yet millions of "snowbirds" flock to this hellscape seeking a better life.

So let's get one thing clear:

Most Americans seek global warming!

No one's moving to Buffalo. No one. Because it's cold and your scrotum will bunjee up to your soft palate if you even think about going outdoors before Cinco de Mayo.

So what's all the fuss about? Bring on global warming. And bring it on *faster*.

Okay, so we lose some slivers of coastline and maybe half of Florida. But by then Alaska will have the same temperature as LA! And the polar bears? They'll adapt, like New Yorkers in Hollywood. All in all, that's a pretty good trade off. So what are you depressed about? The world is okay. You're okay.

It's all *good*.

Q: *But I didn't become rich and famous by the time I was thirty and now I'm going to be turning forty. I mean, why even live?*

A: Awright, awright, Anna Nicole was rich and famous by 27, Belushi by 28, Kurt Cobain by 24 – but look at them now. You're doing great compared to them. You've got *color*.

And hey, maybe it's just me, but I'd rather be alive than be a dead rich and famous person anytime. Personally, I don't need exclusive photos of my shotgun suicide to appear in the National Enquirer in order to feel that I've had a *full life*.

Living, breathing nobodies like yourself have at least a modicum of potential. You're a beautiful if unproven commodity. Paris Hilton we know, and have the grainy video to prove it. But you, who knows what you are – maybe you can sing, maybe you can't. Maybe you're good with puppets or a genius on the pan flute... no one knows, it's just a wonderful mystery,

> *"I got over my depression when I first came upon the strewn bodies at Buchenwald. Now, you can fire me, my wife can go off with a colored man, my kids can marry Jews and I'll still enjoy the day."*
>
> — **General George S. Patton**

like the gentle purr of a kitten (don't laugh, I've been recruited by Hallmark for a six-figure gig).

But the rich and famous, well, they're either in rehab, escaping from rehab, swerving down PCH, or stone-cold dead.

Sheesh... are you kidding? You've already outlived grunge king Cobain by fifteen years, not to mention the scores of celebrities who shuffled off this orb while you took smug comfort in knowing that any one of these deceased demigods would trade places with you in a heartbeat, that is, if they *had* a heartbeat.

Remember, it's not so easy to *not* get killed. There are all sorts of ways you can possibly die but somehow you lived. You beat the odds. You're a winner. And unlike most of the Bee Gees, you really are ah-ah-ah-ah *Stayin' Alive*.

For Chrissakes, take joy in this!

Imagine all the Yuppie blondes on cell phones that could have struck you in the crosswalk and kept on driving to their yoga appointment with your shredded corpse dragging behind their Range Rover.

Or imagine all the diseases you could have picked up at even *one* pro sporting event. If you didn't contract Ebola from that guy in the row behind you — the one wheezing and hacking up those viscous phlegm balls during the entire third quarter of the Jets-Packers game — then you must conclude that God, Jesus, Mohammed and Buddha all have your back.

National Lampoon HELP!

It's an amazing accomplishment. All the drugs you've taken, and didn't take, all the Thanksgivings with the family that didn't end up with your head being blown off by a jealous inbred cousin, your high school that didn't go Columbine, your workplace that didn't go postal.

Cue that overplayed Queen song, because homeboy, you *are* a motherfucking champion!

And it's time you started acting like one instead of the sniveling, whining, pathetic nutcase that you've allowed yourself to become.

In other words, *nut up*.

In Conclusion

Getting the blues can be a normal part of living in modern day America. Sure, little things will bother us, but they need to remain little things. Not getting an Instant Message from your best friend Chaz is not the same as scrounging for scraps of dog meat in the streets of Jakarta. Your life is excellent

Remember, don't be afraid to look at another person's misery and use it to spawn your own personal joy. There must be some good that could come from the great tragedies of life. Let conquering your depression be one of them.

Chapter 9

Organization

In This Chapter...

✔ The upside of Hurricane Katrina

✔ One man's garbage is another man's garbage

✔ Memories are forever if they stay in the landfill.

Decluttering Your Life

It's bad. Random papers, boxes, magazines, wires, broken gear, and the front grill of '74 Chevette litter the once wide open spaces of your abode.

There's crap *everywhere.*

You can't move. Everything is getting smaller. The boxes are growing. There's no where to go. The walls are caving in. Finally you find a narrow landing strip clear of your life's refuse and nestle-in for an afternoon sleep only to overhear a disturbing conversation through your window. It's your landlord downstairs. He's talking to a construction consultant wondering why the apartment building is sinking into the foundation: "I've never seen anything like this. It's as if a herd of elephants were living on the 2nd floor." You look around.

My God, it's *you!*

Get Rid of It!

We've all seen the news stories of the devastation that Hurricane Katrina wrought the people of New Orleans. People standing in their rubble strewn front yards, staring in disbelief at their water ravaged homes – with everything destroyed! Believe it or not, I envy Katrina Victims. Yes I do! I know it sounds incredibly callous and unsympathetic but those poor souls accomplished something very few of us will ever do:

They got rid of their shit!

New Orleans, like it or not, decluttered. They didn't have to make the hard decisions. They didn't have to wade through mountains of worthless crap deciding what lives and what rots in the County Dump. They didn't have to stare for days at a horde of vinyl, trying to determine whether an old Devo LP is a collector's item or just a bunch of weird silly men singing even stranger silly songs that can only be heard using technology developed in the 1870s. It was all done for them. All of it! One Big-Ass Spring Cleaning!

"There's no better way to declutter than having an atomic bomb dropped on your city. It gave us a clear sense of vision and a renewed sense of purpose."
— *Jujiro Matsuda, Founder, Mazda Motors (Hiroshima, Japan)*

Without any thought! All gone! Now that's decluttering! Now that's the *Big Easy!*

Chapter 9: Organization

The Cajun Etch a Sketch has been shaken and cleared and now they can live their lives and start afresh. They are no longer prisoners to their crap — paying sky high mortgages to simply store their life's droppings.

They are FREE!

But not all of us can be as fortunate as to have our crap-warehouse ripped apart by a Cat 5 Hurricane, or flattened by an EF5 Tornado, or leveled in an 8.0 earthquake. No, we have to actually get on our knees for days and perform the excruciatingly long process of heaving our life out.

> *"A man can provide no greater service to his fellow man than to help him declutter"*
> — **Black Beard, Pirate**

So it's not surprising that very few of us have the courage to face this hellish but necessary task.

Like you, I've been holding on to stuff for years, as if one day some scholar from the future is going to rummage through my rat turd infested boxes in search of my 4th grade English papers.

What's that about? Is my ego really that enormous? There's like five guys in the history of the earth that you would ever want to dig through the bottom of their closet — and to tell you the truth, I can't think of one right now! Okay maybe Einstein, but I'm not sure I would want to accidentally encounter his worn out porn cachet.

But me, hey, this stuff is important! How will researchers come to understand the real me without reading my book report on Ole Yeller. How will they ever properly convey the development of my genius without first examining my use of construction paper in my Third Grade map of the USA.

> *"I' can't have clutter, I am in a perpetual state of Clear."*
> — Tom Cruise

You ain't Einstein, no one cares about your old report cards or your Camp Weeqahic Fourth place Ping Pong trophy, that little woodpecker stuffed animal and the bowling pin lamp you made in shop.

I know, it's hard to take but no one's coming down in a space suit in a hundred years sifting through your boxes in an abandoned storage unit. The only one that's coming for your stuff, is a big hungry rat to dump even more feces into the cracks of your old board games.

Here' a wakeup call: the odds are 6 billion to 1 that anyone, including your own children, will ever want to take a dumpster dive in the deep end of your pathetic life. That's pretty much no one – ever! You must get rid of it all!

The only things a person needs are as follows:

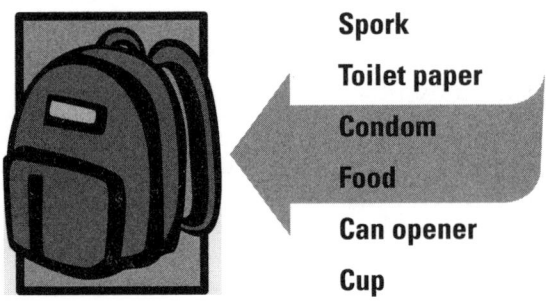

Spork
Toilet paper
Condom
Food
Can opener
Cup

Chapter 9: Organization

Everything else should get the fuck out of your house, now!

What Lives and What Stays

"You know, I can really think in here, even without my $6000 shower curtain."
— Dennis Kozlowski
Former CEO of Tyco and convicted felon

I understand many of us don't have the personal strength or are not quite ready to let go on the level described above. Some of us are still going to hold on to certain items no matter how irrational they are to keep.

That is why I have prepared the following quiz to assist you in making a rational decision on what to keep and what to trash.

Please answer the following questions on any individual item that is cluttering up your life.

1. Have you looked at it more than 3 times in the last 29 years?   Y/N

2. Does it have an odor more foul than a forgotten pair jockey shorts in your gym locker?   Y/N

3. Can you sell it on eBay for more than 4 dollars?   Y/N

4. Does it weigh as much as you after an In & Out run?   Y/N

5. Can it be scrapped for parts?   Y/N

6. Can you still identify its function or purpose?   Y/N

If you answered "Yes" to 2 out of the 6 questions that means you must get rid of it.

However, if you are still not convinced to part with your useless rubbish, then please read the following breakdown of each type of relic that's swallowing you whole.

Cherished video memories

Memories are not photos, they're not videos, they're in our heads! Take your stack of videotapes and crush them – even if they include your wedding video.

No one is watching your wedding video – I have never watched one and have never been invited to watch one.

> *"Why I watched that goddam wedding video I'll never fuck'n know! We separated the next day — son of a bitch!"*
> — Alec Baldwin

And, if you are watching your wedding video, you are going down one spooky path, yes siree. What do you hope to gain by seeing these? Isn't it horrifying enough to see how much you've aged in a photograph, do you need to see a full motion video version of a younger you on the happiest day of your life? What asshole would put himself through such a torture. What is the internal dialogue being played out in your soon to be clinically depressed head:

Chapter 9: Organization

"Wow, look how handsome I was; I'm so happy, we're really in love... Oh my God and now look at me, and that blubbery prune at the other end of the couch"

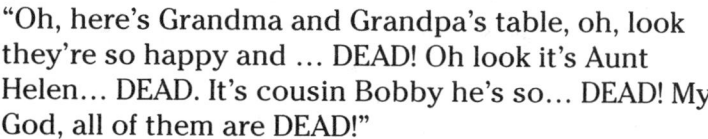

How can this be a good thing?

And it gets worse:

"Oh, here's Grandma and Grandpa's table, oh, look they're so happy and ... DEAD! Oh look it's Aunt Helen... DEAD. It's cousin Bobby he's so... DEAD! My God, all of them are DEAD!"

Who the hell is this self destructive? How depressed does a human being want to get? In fact, if you decide to keep these family event videos, you should be required to place the following warning label on them:

WARNING: YOU ARE ABOUT TO SEE YOURSELF AND ALL YOUR LOVED ONES YOUNG, HAPPY AND ALIVE. THIS MIGHT FREAK THE SHIT OUT OF YOU. WATCH WITH CAUTION. THIS COULD JOLT YOU INTO A WORLD CLASS DEPRESSION AND GET YOU WAY TOO EXISTENTIAL. IF YOU FIND YOURSELF SAYING THE FOLLOWING WORDS: "WHAT'S THE POINT?" "MY GOD YOU REALLY AGE IN THIS WORLD AND PEOPLE DIE" OR "I USED TO FUCK THAT!" TURN IT OFF IMMEDIATELY!

Getting old is supposed to remain human beings collective delusion. We are not supposed mess with this. It's part of our survival that we don't really know that death is just around the corner. It's not something to play with. No one should ever be reminded of their own mortality at this level. Get rid of it!

Every video... get rid of it now!... You are never going to watch it and never should.

I have video tapes of my wife giving birth to my children. I cannot believe this. I was actually coerced into videotaping my son's head popping out of my wife's vaginal cavity! Am I hallucinating? There's no way I actually did this. I nearly vomited on my own newborn kid. Who's watching this?

> *"Birth videos are great. I watch them every night after Seinfeld reruns"*
> — The Zodiac Killer

What sick perverted human being is sitting down watching their children pop out of their wife's vagina? Is that some kind of activity for the next years block party?

What kind of mood do you have to be in to really want to view that revolting bloody mess. Is that a happy mood? A depressed mood? Some kind of odd, pre-suicidal, pre-Virginia Tech rampage kind of mood? If you go to someone's house and they are watching the birth of their children... Just run!

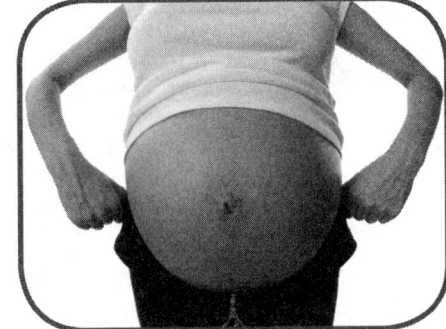

I know parents that have spent most of their time watching their kids life through a camera lens. Who is watching all this footage? There are hundreds of tapes! They need a second life time to watch their first life on tape. Unless you're convinced of reincarnation, it's time to start heaving all of them.

Inferior electronics drawer or closet

The door pops open or you pull the wrong drawer out – and there it is, the never ending pit of electronic has-beens: two cell phones the size of toasters, an old Amiga computer, a fax machine/dot-matrix printer combo, a Sony Discman, a virtual reality headset that made you vomit the last time you fired it up, an Aiwa stereo with all the pretty lights, a spaghetti assortment of cables that can't be plugged into anything that was built after 2000, cheap speaker wire – just a twisted, mangled mess of electronic monstrosities.

And you can only gaze in utter amazement and ask: "Why? Why do I keep these?

What possible reason do I have to continue to provide much prized real estate to house two 17" CRT monitors that are the size of my new Honda Fit. Do they pay rent?"

Are you planning to exhibit them in a museum one day?

What purpose might an actual computer from 1995 serve?

Are you planning on getting nostalgic in a few years for just one more whirl on WordStar? Is there someone alive who's thinking right now, "Man, if only I could have one more shot at a word processor that takes five separate steps to move a block of text!"? No one is craving this… No one! Get rid of it!

Giant cell phones don't help you. Maybe you can use them for skeet shooting or microwaving a Lean Cuisine but that's it. In electronics size does matter: and bigger is not better. Bigger is a sure sign that you've been asleep at the wheel while technology marches on to an ever smaller drummer. Get with the program and toss the crap!

In fact any electronics thicker than this book should be part of the new land fill for the next tract home development. Get rid of all of it.

Random papers

JUNK MAIL: This is one of the great mysteries of life. Something we truly hate and yet curiously can't quite discard. There must be a moment when you realize that you have enough expired Office Depot coupons – and yet you still hold on to them. Why? Do you really need a discount on a 1.5 Mega Pixel camera? And yet they just keep piling up with the expired car wash coupons and Subway coupons. What do you plan to do with these, bind them and create a coupon book for a very cheap time traveler? Create a scrapbook and present it to your cheap son of bitch Uncle Oliver as a retrospective of his penny-pinching life style.

> *"I begged them to throw out my papers, but no one would let me. I know I could have cracked the 'Unified Field Theory' if only I had some space to think."*
> — Albert Einstein

Heave it! Get rid of it!

Credit Card deals with 27% interest rates. You're kidding? Simple rule, any credit card mailers with an interest rate higher than your mother's age – dump it!

Magazines? What do you hope to gain? Sure it's nice to have a collection of Consumer Report magazines dating back to when MTV actually played music but unless you are planning on purchasing a 1989 Toro push mower or contemplating starting a library on consumer activism, it's completely worthless information.

OLD BUSINESS PAPERS: These are my least favorite crap lying around. Scripts never produced, reports no one read, projects never pursued and fuck you letters never sent – it's a museum of failure. And yet there it is, crumpled up in drawers, piled in boxes, strewn on the floor of your car... Burn it all!

Maybe you've got boxes of multiple drafts of the same script you wrote 5 years ago. Call up every studio right now, and tell them that you will sell all your screenplays for $20 or get a swap meet booth with all your scripts and line 'em up on the table. $19 for everything! If you sell 'em at least you can say you're a working writer. Better yet, open up a booth on Sunset Blvd. in Hollywood like a lemonade stand and put up a sign: Unproduced scripts $5 a piece. Jokes $1. Have a grab bag. Just get rid of it.

FOLDERS: Press kits, product information, real-estate developments, for some reason it's difficult to throw out anything that is in a glossy colored folder. However the irony is that anything that comes in a glossy colored folder is absolutely worthless. Basically if you have to make a glossy colored folder and fill it up with fancy colored paper to sell your product – your product SUCKS!

Has anyone ever purchased anything from one of these folders? And yet they just keep handing them out and you keep taking them. You've mistakenly given these worth in your life and a place to reside

Chapter 9: Organization

in the cracks of your couch. And what are they other than someone else's dream packaged a little nicer than your dreams. You don't even have room for your own printed out Power Point presentations, now you've made room for others because they are in a damn glossy colored folder! .. Don't be afraid, grab and heave!

Get rid of 'em!

Old furniture

Chances are your old furnishings weren't that good the first time around; so what are you keeping them for? The white washed Southwest pine bed is never coming back, ever! The Mauve leatherette desk will never be retro.

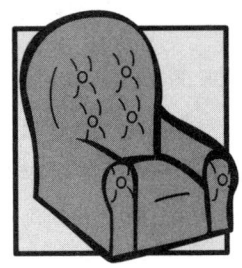

"The way to tell if something is garbage is to hold it up to the light and see if you can see through it. If you can't, it's garbage. If you can, well, wow! That's like totally cool... Wow!"
— Dr. Timothy Leary

Your 1997, Ikea computer desk and matching book case will never rise to the splendor of the Baroque period, nor shall it touch the flowery beauty of Art Nouveau. There's never going to be an Ikea golden age!

It's not going to happen. These are not family heirlooms to be passed down to generation to generation. Your great grandchildren are not going to receive your fake-wood laminate, plastic wheel, with printer shelf, Ikea desk. I know this as fact.

But even if there was, by some fluke, a demand for these popsicle-stick crates, it won't matter – for godsakes they were built by you! – with a prepackaged crescent wrench and plastic nuts& bolts. It wobbled when you first assembled it, it tipped over 3 years ago and it will be dust by the time your grandchild gazes upon it.

"We do get people that come in with their Ikea computer desks but we usually move them into a special area and provide counseling"
— Mark L. Walberg, Host of Antiques Roadshow on PBS

Get rid of it!

Today's Collectibles Are Tomorrow's Trash

Many times people will not throw out something because they are convinced that it will be a collectible one day. However this is an impossible scenario because of the following axiom:

Anything you kept that you perceive may have value in the future is worthless because it's the same crap that everybody else kept and thought would be worth something.

Therefore it is impossible for you to be in possession of a collectible; because if you were, that would mean you threw it out – and consequently not be in your possession.

For example, any rookie cards from 1975 and above aren't worth shit, because everybody held on to them. But before 1975, every mother threw out their kids baseball cards, so those cards are worth something.

You see, the only things that are worth anything, are the things that everybody threw out.

If any of your garbage has any hope of ever being valuable, there must be a massive expunging process – a public clearing-out of that item. But who goes first? And that's the problem. No one wants to be the poor schmuck that threw out his baseball card collection for fear that one day they might be worth a fortune. But yet if they are to be worth something, people need to start tossing. And that's the paradox. And that's why we have more clutter today – because no one wants to be the schmuck.

So we hold onto all this crap out of fear. We're drowning in baseball, football, basketball cards. We're suffocating on signed balls, helmets, and hockey sticks. We're being crushed by old board games and ancient video game systems – we're going to burst!

The solution: GET RID OF IT!

Trust me, throw them out. They'll never be worth anything and they're eating up valuable space that can be used to install your very own Velveeta Nacho Cheese machine. Hell, you can probably build your own food court in the space that these faux collectibles occupy.

And there are other clues to the collectable madness. If you see any of the following words marked on a product – it is a guaranteed stamp of worthlessness.

- ✔ Anything with the word "souvenir" on it
- ✔ Anything with "rookie" boldly printed over the image
- ✔ Anything with the words "Limited Edition" or "Limited Run"
- ✔ Anything with the word "Collectible"

So if you see any of these markings, you can comfortably without fear toss them.

They are signals to other schmucks to hold on to them but you know better now. You know the axiom. It's right to the cans outside.

Real collectibles

Now I'm not advocating holding on to any of this stuff but I guess a single box won't be too bad.

Okay, you want to know the stuff that will be worth something one day: It's all the things that nobody in their right mind would ever keep.

Here's the list of tomorrow's *Real Collectibles:*

- ✔ McDonalds sandwich wrappers
- ✔ A bottle of unused antibiotics
- ✔ Expired or used condoms from the AIDS hysteria days of the 1980's and 1990's
- ✔ Celebrity pizza crust authenticated and numbered
- ✔ Cigarette butts
- ✔ Signed hypodermic syringes used to inject steroids into NFL players
- ✔ This book

In Conclusion

Although most of us will never experience the ease of decluttering by surviving a major natural disaster, we can still face our monsters in the closet with determination, no fear and a large snow shovel. But if somehow you just can't face the inevitable, there's always the simple solution of leaving your front door wide open and inviting people to rob you.

Chapter 10

Sex

In This Chapter...

✔ Holding on for dear life

✔ Having sex with an ugly girl

✔ 72 virgins await!

How to Explode On Your Terms

Life would be so much easier if human beings reproduced like bacteria. One moment you're waiting in line ordering a double chocolate latte and BAM, suddenly you're standing behind a duplicate of yourself. Sure, splitting in two can be a tad disorienting as a reproductive method, but not nearly as bad as having some dominatrix ride you for a half and hour, with your testicles hooked up to a car battery, and you can't remember the safe word.

What the hell *is* Sex?

Roll over, don't talk, put the condom on, take the condom off, I like in the front, shut up, I like it in the rear, around the side, in the front, you don't have an STD?, don't come, not yet, not yet…

"How a man and a woman ever come together and have intercourse is the first great mystery of life; how they ever stop is the second."
— John the Baptist

AHHHHH!

For Godsakes, bacteria don't have to go through this, why should we? Why am I designed to think about sex every 7 seconds of my life? Am I really that important to the continuation of the

> *"Sex, sex, sex enough already. Can't we think about something else for a change?"*
> — Pamela Anderson

human species? I've seen what I've accomplished in my lifetime and to tell you truth, I shouldn't be allowed to reproduce. In fact I don't know anybody that I'm too comfortable with leaving their seed behind. Have you seen us?! Just spend an hour inside a Texas McDonalds in the middle of summer! We're revolting! At least bacteria serve a useful purpose on the planet – they're slowly trying to kill us.

But yet my insatiable appetite for sex is so overwhelming I can barely finish this sentence without clicking over for another free online chat with HandyMandy69.

SEX FACTS:

> When she's a hottie, the average duration of human fornication is 4.5 seconds

> Men think about baseball more than any other sport to keep from climaxing

> Most baseball players think about the fans to keep from climaxing

Chapter 10: Sex

Men need to fornicate with anything and everything. And if we were allowed to do it, most of us probably would. Look what happens when a conquering army arrives in a village. They rape everyone. Why? Because they can!

To give advice on sex to a guy is as hopelessly futile as giving eating advice to a starving African child standing in the middle of a food court. When he spots the Sbarro's he's gone. No game plan, no sampling, just pizza slices until he hurls.

When a guy has an opportunity for sex, the best you can hope for is to try to hold on as long as possible – that's it.

Holding On — The Anti-Sex Fantasy

Look, you've been put through a lot to get to the sex moment: $200 dinner, $500 Valentines Day Gift, and the endless hours making your hair look like you don't care what your hair looks like. You deserve your moment of ecstasy to last slightly longer than a Yaris Commercial.

"Why would I want to hold on any longer than I already do. I've got three more women to sleep with tonight."
— *Wilt Chamberlain*

But it's difficult, especially if you haven't had sex since the first Gulf War.

The Thinking-of-a-Sport Technique

Men are not too creative when it comes to adjusting their Mojo levels during fornication. Most men, in a fit of desperation, think about Baseball to sustain them, but this is a mistake. Watching a bunch of non-descript men standing around in their baseball uniforms waiting to catch a pop fly can be so profoundly boring that you could actually lose your erection and pass out on top of your partner, possibly suffocating her to death – this has happened.

"If it wasn't for baseball I would have never had sex."
— *Yogi Berra*

But it can get even worse:

During your mental scanning of the outfield, your brain, in a desperate attempt to keep you awake, might unconsciously throw in a face or two.

Suddenly your favorite baseball player begins to creep into your anti fantasy – it's Derek Jeter. Something's not right. "Am I having sex with Derek Jeter?" Then panic sets in.

Abort image! Abort image!

Then another face appears: It's Alex Martinez. And another – Abort! But it's too late – the floodgate has broken. It's become the "don't think of the pink elephant in the room." You can't turn it off: Daisuke Matsuzaka giving you a hand job, Barry Bonds sucking your knob, Pedro Martinez sitting on your face smoking a cigarette. It's bad, the more you try to get rid of it, the worse it gets. So you try to go old school: Kirk Gibson's homerun gimping across the bases, but he's

 in drag and you're the third baseman! He grabs you as he rounds third and sandwiches you up against the catcher – oh my God it's Yogi Berra. My God, you're being anally raped by Kirk Gibson as you're anal raping Yogi Berra. It's out of control!!! You suddenly jump out of bed, run out of the house, and drive home wondering what team you really play for.

> *"I like to think of the Rutgers Women's Basketball team. It works every time."*
> — Don Imus

Baseball is bad!

Football is a better choice.

It is the perfect balance of boredom and violent male energy which is essential for a good anti-sex fantasy. And you don't have to worry about the face factor because they've got their helmets on.

Football rivals baseball in the boredom factor with its eternal wait between plays, 2 hour video reviews of disputed calls and the monotonous cheer – Defense!.. Defense!.. Defense!

You'll need this boredom to pull yourself out of climax mode, but unlike with baseball, you can get back from football.

If you feel yourself slipping into a stupor, just pull yourself off the field and head to the sidelines – there you'll find a bevy of world class hotties gyrating wildly in bikinis. The Cheerleader is your best friend, when you need to jolt yourself back to the climactic finish.

"You don't know boring until you've seen 40,000 people dressed in the same colors, sitting in their little chairs doing nothing but eating peanuts & Cracker Jacks. It does the trick every time."

— Hank Aaron

Although football can be boring, it has just enough hard hitting action to keep your mojo levels in check. But don't get too caught up in the testosterone filled action on the field or you may burst too soon. Try to pick a game you can't possibly get into, for instance, a pre-season match up between the Detroit Lions &. The Arizona Cardinals. There is no man on earth that can get into this game, including the player's parents. It is not possible.

Football is one of the better sports to use as an Anti-Sex Fantasy but there are others.

The following is a quick chart of the various sports and how they stack up as Anti-Sex Fantasies.

Due to the lack of information in this unexplored field of human sexuality, please keep this chart with you at all times. Ideally it should be taped to the condom in your wallet.

NATIONAL LAMPOON
ANTI-SEX FANTASY CHART

This quick-reference guide will help you choose the correct sport to delay climax.

SPORT	FACE FACTOR	STUPOR FACTOR	GETTING BACK FACTOR
NASCAR	**Excellent** — Drivers wear crash helmets and are strapped deep inside their car.	**Okay** — After watching a car painted like a box of laundry detergent cruise in circles with a six pack of beer on its tail – you'll only get 3 laps before you lose consciousness. But if you time it right and make it a really short race this could work better than football.	**Decent** — If somehow you can stay awake long enough to make it to the finish line, there will be a gorgeous, blonde honey waiting to give you the trophy and a BJ. Immediately turn your attention back to your sex partner just as she unzips your pants in the winners circle.
SOCCER	**Dangerously Poor** — Bad choice. Soccer players lead with their heads and that Beckham is kind of cute – a guaranteed homo-erotic climax.	**Not Good** — We're Americans, not Manchester United hooligans. To our uncultured sports palate, Soccer is somewhere between watching the Weather Channel and watching your Dad cut his toenails. If you choose this sport, you may never take another breath again.	**Not Possible**

SPORT	FACE FACTOR	STUPOR FACTOR	GETTING BACK FACTOR
FISHING	**Good** — My God have you seen these guys? Even if you do catch a glimpse of a couple of their mugs, they won't register in your libido any more than the carton of worms they're holding or the tackle box.	**Dangerously Poor** — Worse than Soccer — try using the excitement of unhooking a small mouth bass to keep from entering low blood pressure induced cardiac arrest. Warn your partner before using this tactic. Have her place a pillow on her chest to give herself just enough of an air pocket to continue breathing once you collapse on her.	**Unknown** — Your only hope is when you're heading down the tunnel towards the light, the sound of "Clear!" will snap you back into your body with your erection intact — from then on you're on your own.
A TRIP TO THE ZOO (Not a sport but I couldn't help myself)	**Excellent** — Hippos, Elephants, Wildebeests, c'mon can it get any better? I wish I had thought of this the night I got an actual Penthouse Pet in the sack — okay she posed for the magazine 5 years earlier and she was only in a back page spread, well actually more like one of those little ads in the classifieds section, but hey, she appeared in Penthouse… Let's just say the baseball thing didn't work that night — but man, a leisurely mind-stroll through the Bronx Zoo and I would have lasted at least 3 minutes.	**Excellent** — Boring, boring, boring…and yet filled with an air of danger and fascination. Viewing the Elephants & Rhinos endlessly eating straw or the Polar Bears psychotically walking back and forth from one side of the cage to the other will provide the necessary monotony to keep you from targeting on your partner's tramp stamp. However, before your penis turns to mush, the ferocious growl and fierce stare of the Lion will awaken your loins just enough to continue moderate thrusting.	**Excellent** — Head to the antelope exhibit and quickly find the Gazelles — that is some hot tail!!! I'm sure there are stories between the zookeepers. If not the Gazelles, wait a few seconds at the Giraffe exhibit. The male Giraffes are the Ron Jeremys of the zoo. Within moments the females will be mounted and a combined 34 linear feet of sex show will begin. Get out quickly, the female Giraffe pole dancing around the tree can get anyone off while visiting the zoo — if those damn kids with the balloons weren't around.

How to Have Sex with Ugly Girls

You don't ever have to worry about exploding on impact when you're pounding a swamp donkey. Yeah it can be bad, even horrific... but what choice do you have? You're no gift either. Look at you, your unibrow has formed a land bridge to your sideburns! But none of this should stop you from having sex – even if your blind date is a two-bagger.

> *"I'm waiting. Any takers?"*
> — *Condoleeza Rice*

You can never risk falling off your game for when the smokin' hottie arrives. Practice is always good.

And that's where the ugly girl comes in: She's ready, able, and willing to go the distance. Even the greatest athletes get most of their playing time with the practice squads. All week NFL stars are scrimmaging against Third stringers to get ready for the big game on Sunday. Boxers spend 99% of their actual fighting time beating the hell out of their inferior sparring partners as they tune up for the big bout.

You're in training!

And ugly girls are great sparring partners! You can pretty much do whatever the hell you want with them, and they'll show up the next day for more. They're just grateful to be in the ring – with anybody.

Plus, there are other advantages:

- ✔ Absolutely no pressure to perform – even if you're sporting a flab flap over your schlong.

- ✔ Low risk of STDs – hey they don't get out much and neither do you.

- ✔ Can experiment with new positions including having her lowered onto you while she's strapped in a spiked harness, balled and gagged.

- ✔ Can try role playing and you don't have to question how ridiculous you'll look in the Cowboy Chaps – you're just going with it baby because it just doesn't matter.

So how do you do it?

Okay here's the deal: the woman you imagine shacking up with for the long term might look gorgeous today, but in 20 years she's going to look about at the same level as any ugly young one you might shag right now. That's a fact.

And I'm being kind with 20 years, look what happened to Brittany Spears in just two!

> *"Thank God I slept with some ugly women when I was a young man. So it wasn't quite as much of a shock that it could have been."*
> — George H.W. Bush

You may live to 100 (not unrealistic these days) which means that for at least 60 years of your life, you are probably going to be sleeping with an ugly chick. There's just no way around it! And I'm accounting for all her plastic surgery, stomach stapling, and your imminent macular degeneration & cataract problem.

So you might as well get over it sooner rather than later, and enough with the high and mighty bullshit:

"I could never, ever pork a fat chick!"

"I could never do the nasty with a butta face!"

"I could never sleep with my mom!"

Pal, that's pretty much all you're going to be sleeping with, once you get out of your twenties. Get used to it!

Exercise:

Picture the hottest babe you know. Now picture her in 20 or 30 years. Here, let me help you:

Now lock onto that older image of the hottie and compare her to that young chick with the giant head from upstairs that keeps knocking on your door every hour asking you for a cup of sugar.

You see, she's really not that bad. In fact, she's quite lively and fun. And, although it's hard to believe, she's actually hotter than Nicole Kidman will be in 3 years, Cameron Diaz in 6 months and Kathleen Turner the minute after she wrapped production on *Body Heat* in 1981.

Look, we all want to boink the finest tail out there but in reality it's only going to happen maybe a few times in our lives. You need to lower your standards if you're going to stay in the game. Keep in training and when that finer lady emerges, you'll be ready to take her the distance, at least until she morphs into Janet Reno.

If All Else Fails There is Always Jihad

A few years ago, we did a piece for *nationallampoon.com* entitled "The 72 Virgins Terrorists Might Find in Heaven." Recently, it was proposed that we turn this piece into a small novelty book. Our publishing division agreed, but wanted assurances that the satire be aimed at insane Islamic extremists and not at the vast majority of so called "moderate Muslims," the reasonable ones who no doubt rejected this whole 72 virgins thing. Well, I decided to research this on the Internet, and to my surprise struggled to find any mainstream Muslim organizations that rejected this sex-for-death-for-Allah conviction.

Convinced they were out there, I went deeper with my research, even more determined to find some Imam on the internet that found this belief to be repulsive – but along the way something strange happened to me, I became obsessed with the 72 Virgins.

And what I discovered was a revelation.

The 72 virgins are called the "Black Eyeds" because of their stunning black eyes. But more importantly (at least for me) are their enormous, upright, perky breasts. And it gets better: they are completely submissive, willing to fulfill the nastiest sexual fantasy any dead Jihadist can muster.

And of course:
There are 72 of them and they're all young virgins!

Page after Internet page of descriptive, sultry accounts of the "Black Eyes." Any notion of publishing a book or whatever I was doing was supplanted by a much greater need – to wank it. Within 15 minutes, I had to visit TheHun.com (my Mecca of Internet porn) but there was not one link that could reach the perverted sexual imagery that my "research" was spawning in my loins. Screw the Hun! I needed more research! I couldn't get enough. I must have hit twenty Muslim sites, reading, researching, and masturbating.

I was out of control!

Imagine seventy-two young women (we'll leave age out of this), licking every part of your body and serving your every need. It became my new fetish. I tried the sandwich position, lining up 36 virgins and having them bend over while 36 others laid underneath. I put myself in a golf cart with the front seat facing sideways, and one extra virgin driving for me and had intercourse with each of the Black Eyes' directly from the golf cart.

Last night I had the girls in a conga line, wearing strap-ons, all connected, dancing over me while I lay on my back. God or Allah, please help me! But it didn't stop...

Chapter 10: Sex   181

Wow! I can't wait to die, and I'm Jewish. This must happen to me. I must have this. And to think: all I need to do is blow myself up.

And it could happen for you.

Come on. Life isn't really that great. You get maybe a half an hour each day to do anything, and we usually spend it surfing Internet porn anyway. So what are we waiting for? Are we all nuts? This is the greatest gig ever!

Blow yourself up for *seventy two grade-A pussies.*

These Muslims aren't crazy. They're the sanest people on Earth. You want crazy? The Japanese. They're fuckin' nuts. The kamikaze pilots who flew their planes into American ships, blowing themselves up for honor? What the hell's that about? I wouldn't trade my foreskin for honor. Thank God the Imperial Emperor of Japan didn't throw in the seventy-two

"I had 72 virgins in one night but I wouldn't say it was paradise, more like an average day."
— **Wilt Chamberlain**

virgin thing or we would all be driving Toyotas (hey, wait a minute). Yeah, a couple nukes and the whole honor thing is forgotten, but seventy-two virgins? There are not enough hydrogen bombs on Earth to quell that male fantasy.

Convert to Islam and become a martyr!

Although the benefits of martyrdom are clear, you'll need to get some assurances from your local Iman before pushing the button. Make sure your Muslim cleric agrees to the following:

- ✔ I will get the Black Eyes
- ✔ They do anal.
- ✔ At least half are lesbians.
- ✔ Props will be available (whips, handcuffs, anal invader, golf cart, etc).
- ✔ They won't talk back – unless part of a fantasy or shouting the safe word.
- ✔ No condoms.
- ✔ No STD testing.
- ✔ If I fail in my mission (to murder the infidel) I still get to go to Paradise

Chapter 10: Sex   183

> *"It's not the blowing up that bothers me, it's how uncomfortable the vest is, I can barely breath under it."*
>
> — Osama bin Laden

Okay, that last one seems like a stretch but my research indicates that even the clumsy jihadists get to go – look it up. They're always blowing themselves up before they reach their target: lighting the wicks too early, scratching that nasty itch under the death vest with an extra stick of C4… and still it's considered that they martyred themselves. Does it get any better? You don't even have to murder anybody (other than yourself) to make it to your own personal Chicken Ranch in the sky.

NATIONAL LAMPOON DOES NOT ADVOCATE MURDER IN THE NAME OF JIHAD. HOWEVER IF YOU ARE WILLING TO BLOW YOURSELF UP AND NO ONE GETS HURT (EXCEPT YOU) AND YOU GET TO BONE 72 PRIME-ASS VIRGINS FOR ETERNITY – WELL WE'RE NOT GOING TO STOP YOU.

In Conclusion

It's sad that the only sure way to have ultimate sexual bliss is to murder yourself and quite possibly innocent civilians. However, maybe we weren't supposed to have our wildest sexual fantasies fulfilled.

Maybe we're supposed to have just enough sexual angst that it makes us want to get up in the morning and pursue life.

Imagine a world without a sex drive. Would we ever tolerate the other gender unless we needed to have intercourse with them? As soon as they would hassle us for watching five NFL games in a row – that would be the end of it. Why would we ever bother?

There would be no big cars produced or tall buildings constructed to show the world our manhood or lack thereof. There would be no nice clothes, no haircuts, no breath mints. There would be no economy. And ultimately no real point to being alive. But yet here we are tortured, miserable that we can't be Brad Pitt for a day. Maybe it's God's design that most of us are Jack Black because in the final analysis it's more rewarding

Chapter 11
Living In The Moment

In This Chapter...

✔ Mental illness: The Great Liberator

✔ Choosing the psychosis that's right for you

✔ A doctor's note for behaving badly

Enlightenment Through Affliction

You hear it all the time. Friends, family, and the media are constantly encouraging us to "Seize the Day." Are we supposed to take this "zen" shit seriously? How can we ever hope to live in the ever present *now* when mainstream culture places needless and suffocating social barriers upon us?

"Don't run! Don't step on the lawn! Don't feed the ducks!"

Don't shout during Yom Kippur services, "Am I the only one who's fucking hungry here?!"

Don't stand up at a Democratic Party fundraiser and scream, "When are you Commies going to start making my life easier!"

...or at a Republican Party dinner,

"Why am I here? Doesn't Halliburton and Texaco pick up the tab for all this crap?!?"

We'd like to say and do these things, but of course we can't. The meaningless rules and conventions that plague our society are a stark reminder that despite the promise of freedom we are not truly free to live in the moment.

> *"It was my eating disorder that really allowed me to be one with the universe. People saw my big fat belly and felt sorry for me, and I went with it."*
> — The Buddha

Our country was founded on the idea of freedom yet we are not free to follow our natural impulses and pursue life with the devil-may-care abandon that our Founding Fathers no doubt intended.

That is, of course, unless you acquire an affliction.

A Good Mental Disorder is the Key to Life

The most liberated people in our society have benign mental disorders that allow them to display an array of so called "socially unacceptable behaviors" without facing any consequences.

A simple diagnosis of ADHD, or Attention Deficit Hyperactive Disorder, is a free ride to uninhibited debauchery. Anything goes. Basically you are out-of-fucking-control and it's okay because you have a *doctor's note.*

> *"I mean, it is just so unfair that I can't scream "fire" in a crowded movie theatre. Do I ever get a chance to have fun?"*
> — George Lucas

It's kind of like Tourette's Syndrome but with your "episodes" spread out across every waking moment. And there's nothing anybody can do to stop you. It's legal, state-sanctioned permission to behave like Kim Jong-Il but without the nukes.

> "One day, there will be no hall monitors and assistant principals and I'll truly be free!"
> — John Belushi (Age 14)

For example, if you're in a college classroom and listening to an endless, droning lecture about the *metabolic pathways of plant life*, you can suddenly spring up out of your chair and scream: "For the love of God, my testicles itch!"

No amount of New Age voodoo is going to allow you to be that *"present."*

Now when I was a kid, if you displayed any symptoms of ADHD, sooner or later someone would beat the hell out of you and that was the end of it.

Mercifully, those days are long gone. Because now...

Being a jackass is an actual disease!

It's true. You're sick. You are a *special needs* person!

With an ADHD diagnosis and two or three lawyers to defend you, you are completely unstoppable. There is no need that can't be fulfilled, no thirst that can't be quenched. You are pure "ID."

We all crave this freedom. This past weekend, I was test driving a Prius Hybrid (I live in LA and need to keep up appearances, but that's another story). As I was pulling out of the dealership, I was suddenly overcome with a tremendous urge to steer into the large water pond and fountain that graced the front of the dealership.

National Lampoon **HELP!**

This impulse was motivated by a sudden desire to know if it's possible to electrocute myself (and the hapless salesman in the passenger seat) by driving an electric vehicle into a towering wall of water. I can't explain this dangerous and utterly pointless quest for useless information, but the urge was very real. Just for the record, I didn't do it.

But what if?

> "I owe my life to hyperactivity and I owe my hyperactivity to Pixie Sticks."
> — Tom Arnold

What if I had that doctor's note — that wonderful ADHD badge of freedom? Armed with this legal license to thrill, I would have aimed right for that goddam fountain, sparks flying, salesman in full cardiac shock and me laughing satanically all the way to oblivion. And if I had somehow lived and remained conscious, when the cops and news vans arrived I would have grinned broadly and presented to them...*a note from my doctor.*

What are they going to do? It's expected of me. I might even get a little sympathy. Maybe one of the cops would inquire into the results of my little experiment. When the news broke, I might be asked to write an article about it for Popular Mechanics. It could happen!

Anyway, you get the point. It's amazing how much we actually hold back in life because we don't have an official diagnosis, or a special placard dangling from our rear view mirror alerting the world of our malady so they can get the hell out of the way.

Chapter 11: Living in the Moment **191**

Like right now I have the impulse to take off my clothes and run stark naked through the halls of the National Lampoon offices, firing ballistic turds out of my butt and screaming, *"No more 3D animated movies featuring insipid photorealistic woodland creatures!"*

But I don't. I can't. I need an *affliction* to follow my bliss.

Picking Your Mental Affliction

Today, nearly everyone can find a mental disorder that suits their personality and impulses. But this wasn't always the case.

A couple of decades ago, repressed free spirits had little to work with except the then-popular *dyslexia*

"SPECIAL NEEDS" FACTS

> Woody Allen, an OCD sufferer, married his own wife's daughter... now that's living in the moment, baby!

> Alec Baldwin suffers from OCD and apparently can't say anything too outrageous that will keep him from booking his next job.

> Danny Glover, an ADHD sufferer, publicly stated that if Osama bin Laden is captured, his life should be spared... and he still got to be in *Dream Girls*.

and *hyperactivity* syndromes. It was a challenge. Dyslexia was just too limiting. Sure you were excused from reading *Moby Dick* and finishing your report on Calvinism, but you still couldn't just rip a 100 decibal fart in class and then point wildly in every direction while shrieking to your horrified teacher and classmates, "He who smelled it dealt it!" Not without getting "Progress Reports" sent to your parents for the rest of your natural life.

Now c'mon, that's not exactly living in the moment.

"I hjad Disxia and gfot tdo rrubb my pqeniss acainst Mray Smmiht"s leg druing Mtath'. Noo plnblem! It wsa aowsme !!!"
— *Alexder Grham Blle;l"*

Hyperactivity was a little better. It allowed for flashes of pure vitriol, and near-violent reactions in any public setting. However, it only worked if you appeared to be in a continuous and "chittery" state of hyper-ness.

And that's the problem.

The *faux* hyperactive had to maintain the constant illusion of being a kid who had just knocked off an entire bag of Halloween candy or drank twelve Jolt colas in an hour. Any outburst or rage that spewed forth from a relatively normal state would invite a good ass-whooping.

Oh but today, in the glorious modern world, you are feted to a veritable *Hometown Buffet* of scrumptious mental disorders. To name but a few:

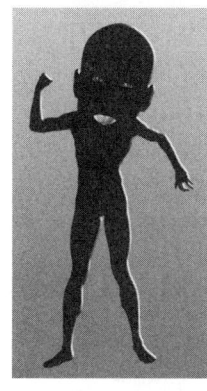

- ✔ **OCD** — *Obsessive Compulsive Disorder*
- ✔ **ADD** — *Attention Deficit Disorder*
- ✔ **APD** — *Anti Personality Disorder*
- ✔ **ODD** — *Oppositional Defiant Disorder*

    ...and of course my favorite,

- ✔ **ADHD** — *Attention Deficit Hyperactive Disorder*

Granted, some of these mental states may be hard to fake for extended periods of time, so let's examine just those that are more or less *effortless* and can be turned on or off at will.

"The greatest day of my life was when my doctor said I suffering from ODD, or Oppositional Defiant Disorder...even though the asshole doctor was wrong! They always think they're God, don't they? Well, fuck him!"
— *Paula Abdul*

In addition to ADHD, which we've covered, let's consider two additional liberating disorders...

Post Traumatic Stress Syndrome

This label was created for distraught Vietnam Vets returning from the horrors of armed combat and the futility of a war that couldn't be won. But what if your late-mid-century birth date caused you to miss action in Da Nang by a decade or two?

As luck would have it, the clinical definition of PTSS has now been expanded to include anybody who has ever crashed and burned in pursuit of a noble if ultimately tragic pursuit. Basically, if you've ever been in a bad relationship, a failed business, or you're a Cubs fan, you're entitled to the same diagnosis as that fucked-up homeless vet in the flak jacket on the corner of Fifth and Main. It's that easy.

And once you have that golden *doctor's note,* you can go absolutely ape-shit: scream, shout, get murderously depressed, walk around with signs claiming the end of the world, piss in the street, yell "motherfucker! motherfucker! motherfucker!" a thousand times an hour. It's life in the purest moment without the dread of a single consequence — and you are one with the universe.

> *"Now that I've played out the drug addiction angle, next year I'm going to choose Anti-Personality Disorder. Yep, APD should do the trick."*
> — Robert Downey Jr.

Obsessive Compulsive Disorder

We've all seen the *Dateline NBC* and *20/20* reports where an obsessed germophobe can't stop washing his or her hands, but did you know that OCD can be applied to *any* behavior that is practiced to the point of compulsion? Now who doesn't have *that* illness? I can't stop watching the Buffalo Bills, even though most years they suck. I can't explain it, I know it's wrong, but it's what I have to do every Sunday.

> *"People think I'm a huge Laker fan, but I'm a bigger fan of OCD. That's why I never miss a game."*
> — Jack Nicholson

An OCD diagnosis will guarantee you a world of endless joy. Any weird or shameful behavior that was once kept hidden can now be publicly exhibited and explained away as OCD.

"I can't stop calling you, because of my OCD."

"I can't study for my test because I can't stop watching television...It's my OCD."

"I wish I could help you move, but my OCD is really bad today and I can't stop looking at web sites with the words Thai and Teen in them."

"Nice rack, can I have a feel? Nice rack, can I have a feel? Nice rack, can I have a feel?"

In the context of your perceived illness, the socially unacceptable is now acceptable. You can thumb your nose at the time-honored social conventions of the world, and the world will understand... it's your OCD.

Your Official ID & Permission Slip

It's important that you occasionally mention your chosen affliction at the office, corner bar, house of worship, or any place that you frequent on a regular basis. This way people will be prepared for your *"in-the-moment"* lifestyle.

However, for those times when you absolutely *must* rant in the presence of strangers, you may be required to flash some form of documented proof of your affliction, if only to avoid a slap in the face, a kick in the nuts, or worse, a summons.

I recommend that you fill out the following form and carry at least one copy with you at all times. You should *never* leave home without these credentials.

This is your ticket to every man's dream of ultimate freedom.

TO WHOM IT MAY CONCERN:

Please excuse _____
for the following inappropriate outburst or threat (circle one or more):

"Show me your tits!"

"Are those real?!"

"Sit on my face!"

"Ugh! Do you always smell like that?!"

"Are you dying or is that how you normally look?"

"AAAAAAAAAAAAAAHHHHH!"

"Does anybody fuckin' work here?!"

"Hey asshole, get the fuck out of the teller line before I rip that checkbook in half!"

"Ouch! Why the fuck are you giving me an anal search when the guy behind me is speaking Arabic and looks like Osama bin Laden?"

"Get a goddam hair cut, you asswipe. I can't see!"

"You suck as a CEO!"

"Fuck you, I'm not leaving until I'm full. The signs says All You Can Eat!"

"Get these kids outta the way so I can slide down the goddam tube already!"

"Can I have $10,000?"

"You're not real, you're just big and ugly."

"Sweet Mary, Mother of God! Were you always that fat?"

"Wow! You are so bald!"

"I have to press this green button! I have to press this green button!"

"Please have sex with me and my wife!"

"What the hell does this have to do with anything in the real world?"

"Stop the wedding, she's just too ugly!"

"Can someone please close the casket? This is disgusting!"

"Lets bury the bitch already."

"I don't care how many trophies he's won, your kid sucks at baseball!"

"Fuckin-A, you are the hottest teacher in this school."

"How can I pay attention when your nipples are about to launch through your bra?"

Other_____

Other_____

He has been diagnosed with a disabling mental disorder known as:

_____

Although his conduct can appear troubling, please know that he is completely harmless. Do not be afraid. If you have any questions or concerns please look up the disorder on Wikipedia.com or run very fast.... Now! What are you waiting for – Go!

Sincerely,

Dr. Scott Rubin, Ph.D
**Department of Psychiatric Studies
The National Lampoon Institute**

In Conclusion

Living in the Moment is man's God-given right. No chains, no laws, no social mores should ever keep him from acting on his impulses – no matter how outrageous and troubling.

Thanks to Freud, we finally have our freedom!

So live in the moment and run to your doctor... Fuck writing! It's just so damn hard and it takes forever! Why do I have to write these goddamn conclustion paragraphs anyway? – Just because the art director formatted the book that way! Screw him, I'm the author and I don't want it.

Well, yeah. Sorry.

You see, I actually have a note with me... you see, I suffer from a mental affliction known as ADHD, well, it's all right here. Just take a look.

Chapter 12
The Search For God

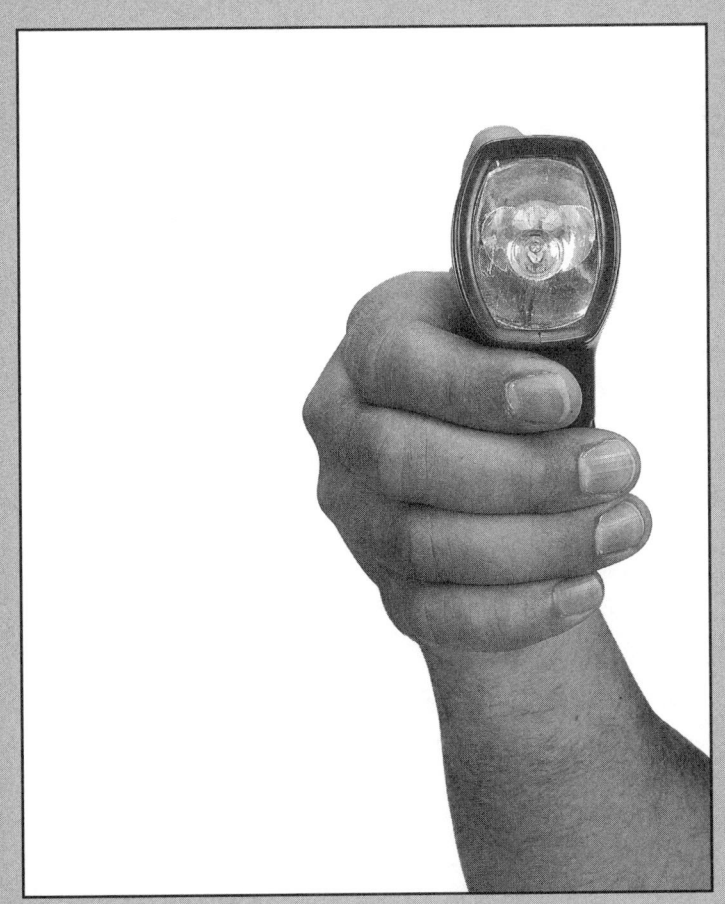

In This Chapter...

✔ Bottoming out beats praying

✔ Partying hard to find the Lord

Finding The Lord Almighty

I would be doing a great disservice if I didn't address the search for God.

So many of us feel so alone, disconnected and out of touch. We yearn to be connected to something bigger than ourselves. We look and we look but yet the infinite spirit seems so unattainable, if it even exists at all. Is this all there is? Is life just a Big Mac and a Large Fries? I mean two Big Macs, a Large Fries, Fillet O' Fish, Chicken McNuggets and a Large Coke. Isn't there something more?

Yes there is! And you can feel the same deep connection with the Lord just like the many guests that have testified to his divine, unconditional love on the *700 Club*.

You can have it. And the good news is that you're already half way there – you just need to amp up the volume a bit on your lifestyle.

You see, the secret to finding God is, (drum roll please) is really no secret at all. In fact, every day on religious television, guests quiver in tears as they describe exactly how it happens:

They *"bottomed out."*

> *"To search for the almighty is futile, but if on that journey you happen to be hit by a car at 60mph, your odds radically increase."*
> *— Mahatma Ghandi*

And it's pretty much the same story with everyone. A person going through life starts drinking, smoking, cavorting, gorging and then one day they find themselves face down in the street in a pool of their own vomit. Then, a miracle happens and God surrounds them in light and they are saved by his unimaginable love.

That's it. Of course there are slight variations to the tale: sometimes it's too much eating, sometimes it's too much sex, sometimes it's too many drugs, but eventually the person will end up in their own puke on the side of road.

It's the closest we're ever going to get to empirical evidence: Thousands of people from all walks of life with pretty much the same story.

Therefore...

The Easiest Way To God Is To Bottom Out

"God, God, God, been there, done that."
— Lindsay Lohan

Now there are no guarantees but it's as rock solid a way to get to God that you'll ever find. All you have to do is just bottom out. Do you realize how close you are already to this? I mean, with a little nudge and a push, you can be face to face with the Almighty in no time! How great is that? And the best part is, you can accomplish this with none of that religious mumbo jumbo stuff.

"It's always about you."
— Me

Think about it: No conversion classes, no reborn again revivals, no million man marches, no blowing yourself up, no wearing funny fur hats & not driving on Saturdays, no embarrassing moments having your naked body plunged into a pool of water, no studying cryptic tomes for decades. None of it, just simply destroy your life in a 3- week party binge! You were going to do this anyway, now just add another couple of weeks to it. And don't forget, you must bring yourself to the brink of an early death.

Let's get busy in the name of the Lord!

In this section, we'll review all the ways you can bottom out by sheer excess and find yourself closer to God.

But first, this disclaimer:

NATIONAL LAMPOON AND THIS AUTHOR (THAT WOULD BE ME – SCOTT RUBIN) CAN NOT PROMISE THAT YOU WILL MEET GOD BY TAKING THE FOLLOWING ADVICE. IN FACT YOU MAY END UP MEETING SOMETHING FAR MORE SINISTER.

IT IS ALSO POSSIBLE THAT YOU WILL JUST DIE A TERRIBLE AGONIZING DEATH WITH ABSOLUTELY NO SENSE OF THE DIVINE PRESENCE OR DEMONIC INTRUSION. BASICALLY YOU'LL JUST DIE AND ENTER A GREAT VOID OF NOTHINGNESS.

OH AND THIS BOOK IS PARODY, SATIRE, COMEDY AND HUMOR. IF YOU TAKE THIS ADVICE OR ANY INSTRUCTION IN THIS BOOK SERIOUSLY YOU PROBABLY DESERVE TO DIE A PREMATURE DEATH – NOT THAT I WISH THAT ON ANYONE, OF COURSE.

Chapter 12: The Search For God

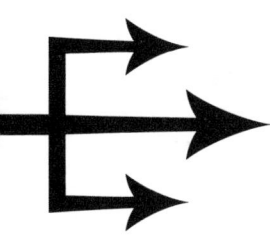

National Lampoon *HELP!*

Chapter 12: The Search For God 207

~~essenibh eros accum dolore velendiam. blaorpero odolorper ipit, quis non eum velisi ex essenibh eros accum dolore velendiam.min utat, valla facillut ea facilla cortie tin vel ipit esequat. Obore tat. Essisim voloreet, conulpa tationsecte n~~

> Why is all this type blacked out?
>
> Here's the skinny: I've been advised by National Lampoon attorneys that I cannot list the ways to achieve a full life collapse.
>
> But I promise you, if you truly follow the lessons from the previous chapters and simply up the dosage slightly, you should be very close to death in a matter of weeks.

In Conclusion

God awaits those who are good people who fall way out-of-bounds a little too early. If the lessons in this book don't result in hastening a life altering big crash, you can always move to Baghdad, lay in the sun everyday without sunscreen while having unprotected anal sex with an Iraqi male prostitute in an open air street market. If that doesn't work, you're immortal.

Now get partying, God awaits!

Scott Rubin

Scott Rubin is the Editor-in-Chief of National Lampoon. Rubin's tenure began in 1999, when he created the award-winning National Lampoon Dotcom as an outlet for the NatLamp's cutting edge comic sensibility. The site's content was entered into the Smithsonian Institute for best exemplifying American satire in the weeks following the 9-11 attacks, and has been awarded "Best of the Web" from the *Los Angeles Times*, *Forbes*, *USA Today*, CNN, *The Wall Street Journal*, and *Entertainment Weekly*. In his eight years running the website, Rubin has created, written or produced nearly 600 pieces including several top ranked YouTube videos. Rubin's brainchild "Seinfeld: The Lost Episode" was one of the top viral videos on the web of 2006 and was featured in *The New York Times*, RollingStone.com, *New York Magazine* and *The Chicago Tribune*.

Mr. Rubin recently co-authored the first title from National Lampoon Press, *National Lampoon The Saddam Dump*. The title landed on numerous recommended lists for humor including: About.com and *Toronto Globe & Mail*. In addition, Rubin has served as editor and contributor for *National Lampoon's Big Book of Love*, and *National Lampoon's Big Book of True Facts*. Rubin is the recipient of the Parents Choice Award, Interactive Arts & Sciences Award and has been nominated for the Webby Award twice.

Rubin is originally from Buffalo, NY and received his BFA in Cinema from the University of Miami. He currently resides in Los Angeles with his family and his undying love for the Buffalo Bills.

Also From
National Lampoon Press

 **National Lampoon Jokes, Jokes, Jokes Collegiate Edition**
Steve Ochs
Mason Brown
978-0977871-827
Price: $11.95 US

 **National Lampoon The Saddam Dump Saddam Hussein's Trial Blog**
Scott Rubin
MoDMaN
978-0977871-858
Price: $14.95 US

 **National Lampoon Favorite Cartoons Of The 21st Century**
National Lampoon Staff And Contributors
978-0977871-810
Price: $14.95 US

 **National Lampoon Not Fit For Print**
National Lampoon Staff And Contributors
978-0977871-834
Price: $17.95 US

 **National Lampoon Road Trip USA**
Harmon Leon
978-0978832308
Price: $15.95 US

 **National Lampoon Van Wilder Guide to Graduating College In Eight Years or More**
MoDMaN
And National Lampoon Contributors
978-0978832-339
Price: $12.95 US

 **National Lampoon Magazine Rack**
Ed. by
J. Naughton
MoDMaN,
P. Cummin
978-0977871-803
Price: $17.95 US

 **The 29th Anniversary of National Lampoon's Animal House**
Chris Miller
978-0978832-346
Price: $12.95 US

AMEX: NLN

NATIONAL LAMPOON's
BAG BOY

The competitive sport of grocery bagging needs a hero.

"Very, very funny script. Fresh and original."

Peter & Bobby Farrelly (Something About Mary, Shallow Hal, Dumb & Dumber)

Get Your Bag On!
In Theaters Summer 2007
DVD Fall 2007